Biking and Hiking the American River Parkway

A Cultural and Natural History Guide

Proceeds from the sale of this guide benefit the nature programs of the American River Natural History Association (ARNHA). ARNHA provides environmental education to children and adults at the Effie Yeaw Nature Center and Preserve and throughout the Sacramento community. ARNHA is an all-volunteer, privately-funded, nonprofit organization formed in 1981.

Fourth revised edition 2011
Third revised edition 2001
Second revised edition 1998

ISBN: 1-887815-16-3

Cover art by Molly Keller
Printed by Delta Web
The American River Natural History Association
P.O. Box 241
Carmichael, CA 95609

Fourth Revised Edition Acknowledgments

This new, updated 4th edition of *Biking and Hiking on the American River Parkway* describes numerous sections of trail, restrooms, emergency telephones, and other enhancements to the Parkway since the original volume was published in 1998. In preparing the new, updated 4th edition, we are most in debt to Robin Donnelly, who created this guide in the beginning. In addition, special thanks go to John Whelan, longtime parkway bicycle commuter who updated the maps; to Jim Michaels, Sate Parks Senior Park and Recreation Specialist who edited Chapters 6 and 7; to Steve Flannery, former Chief Sacramento County Park Ranger; to Chief Park Ranger Kathleen Utley; to Guy Kolling, Associate County Parks Landscape Architect; to John Havicon, Sacramento County Park Ranger; to Molly Keller, who created the art work on the cover; to Katie Baygell for information on equestrian trails and staging areas; to members of the American River Natural History Association Publications Committee for their support and advice; and, most of all, to Dan Lombard, who guided us through the production process. Without his expertise and generous help, this new edition would not exist.

Co-editors Peggy Kennedy and Pete Hayes, 2011

Acknowledgements

Biking and Hiking the American River Parkway is a product of the American River Natural History Association (ARNHA) for the community of Sacramento. Many people shared their time, skill and memories of special people and places. Among these are Greg Voelm, Doug Grant, Fred Gunsky, Jo Smith, Mary Trudeau, Helen Mills, Randy Smith, Gail Mackenroth, Carol Doersch, Wendy Anderson, Paula and Fred Baldi, Sandy Hunt, Jack Hiehle, Don Bergst, Norm Wilson, Eric Warp, Judi Kusnick, Erin, Chris, Meghan and Tom Donnelly and, production specialist, Sarah Toll. Thanks also go to the County of Sacramento Department of Regional Parks, Recreation and Open Space, especially Rangers Thom Oliver, Jane Browne, and John Havicon; Director Sue Wittorff and the Effie Yeaw Nature Center staff; and California State Park Ranger, Rick LeFlore. Generous and knowledgeable access to archives was provided by Jim Henley, Charlene Noyes, and Patricia Johnson of the Sacramento History and Science Archives; June Hose and Julie Bowen of the Folsom History Museum; and Tom Hickey, of the Folsom Prison Museum. Two ARNHA publications, *The Outdoor World of the Sacramento Region* and *The History of the Lower American River,* provided additional background.

Photos are the creative gifts of Randy Smith and David Rosen. Illustrations were graciously provided by Erin O'Toole and Jo Smith. The book cover was created by Deborah Rasmussen. The map was patiently prepared by Bjorn Gregersen of Sugnet & Associates, the American River Parkway Foundation and ARNHA.

Special thanks to Directors Gene Andal, Gary Kukkola, and Deputy Director Roy Imai with County of Sacramento Department of Regional Parks, Recreation and Open Space, whose efforts keep open space and recreation opportunities available for all to enjoy.

Creating and making full use of this guide calls for both an active body and an active mind. We wish you many hours of enjoyment.

Happy trails,

Robin Donnelly, author, 1988

The creation of the American River Parkway took time, money, and the commitment and cooperation of a wide range of people and organizations. This effort is continuing today.

Parkway Support Organizations

The **American River Natural History Association** (ARNHA) "brings nature to people and people to nature." This all-volunteer, privately funded, non-profit educational organization funds and manages the Effie Yeaw Nature Center, conducts school programs, and provides workshops and publications. www. sacnaturecenter.org, www. ARNHA.org, and 916-489-4918.

The **American River Parkway Foundation** (ARPF) provides Parkway support, fosters environmental stewardship, and facilitates volunteer opportunities through programs such as Adopt the Parkway, Down River Day, and the Great American River Clean-up. www.arpf.org and 916-486-2773.

The **Save the American River Association** (SARA) is the political arm of the Parkway triad. Founded in 1961 to spearhead the establishment of the American River Parkway and adoption of the Parkway Plan, the volunteer non-profit works to ensure that the American River Parkway will survive and prosper for the benefit of future generations. www.sarariverwatch.org and 916- 482-2551.

Sacramento Valley Conservancy (SVC) preserves the beauty, character and diversity of the Sacramento Valley landscape by working with citizens, property owners, developers, public agencies, and other nonprofit organizations to preserve dedicated open space. sacramentovalleyconservancy.org.

The **American River Parkway Volunteer Equestrian Trail Patrol** promotes safety in the use of parkway property and facilities. arphorsepatrol.org.

SOME ADDITIONAL GROUPS:

The **Sacramento Audubon Society** offers expert bird walks in the Parkway. Its Checklist of the Birds of the Sacramento Area is an indispensable guide. www. sacramentoaudubon.org.

The **Sacramento Tree Foundation** offers tree planting in the Sacramento Area, including the American River Parkway. www.sactree.com and 916-924 -8733

The **California Native Plant Society** offers educational botanical trips in the Parkway. www.CNPS.org and 916-447-2677.

The **Friends of the River** is California's largest river conservation organization. www.friendsoftheriver.org and 916-442-3155.

BIKING AND WALKING CLUBS:

The **Sacramento Area Bicycle Advocates** (SABA) seek to improve acceptance of bicycling for transportation and lobby for commuter access points and bicycle trails. www.sacbike.org.

The **Sacramento Bike Hikers**, Sacramento's oldest bicycle club with nearly 700 members, focuses on touring and recreational cycling. They sponsor trail rides throughout the area, including the American River Parkway. Most bicycle shops have the schedule of rides and membership applications. www.bikehikers.com.

The **Sacramento Wheelmen** schedule rides on weekdays, weekends, and over multiple days. The majority of rides are for road bikes, but they also offer mountain bike rides and self-contained tours. They sponsor the annual Sierra Century, a premier cycling event in northern California. www.sacwheelmen.org .

Sierra Race Walkers is a California non-profit organization promoting the amateur sport of race walking. wwww.sierraracewalkers.org .

Sacramento Walking Sticks sponsors non-competitive walks in association with the American Volkssport Association. Founded in November 1984, the group sponsors events open to the public. www.sacramentowalkingsticks.org.

Table of Contents

About the Biking and Hiking Guide

Biking and Hiking the American River Parkway is a guide to the natural and cultural history of the 32-mile Jedediah Smith Memorial Bicycle Trail. Many of the animals, places, and trails described were familiar to Nisenan, the native tribe of the southern Maidu, fur trappers, explorers, pioneers, gold miners, Pony Express riders, railroad men, and settlers. For the last hundred years, bicycling and hiking enthusiasts like yourself have shared in the adventure. The guide is designed so that you can begin your journey at any location.

Information about the trail is presented in seven chapters, each describing a section of the trail, unique stops, sidetrips, and convenient access points. Detailed maps precede each section. New in this edition, on pages xii and xiii, is detailed information about horse staging areas, and icons mark horse staging areas on all section maps. As the text follows the trail in a "west to east" direction, the term "up the trail" means farther east, or upriver. Mileage readings and the maps will help you if you are using the guide traveling the opposite direction. An odometer comes in handy but is not necessary. Miles are marked on the trail and on occasional "You Are Here" maps.

USING THE GUIDE

Text in this type gives details about side trips and closer looks. When a plant or animal is illustrated it is identified by bold type in the text. **Symbols identify the following:**

- Side Trip
- Closer Look
- Restaurants
- Picnic Tables
- Restroom
- Portapotty
- Public Telephone
- Emergency Telehone
- Parking
- Drinking Fountain
- Access
- Horse Staging Area
- Bicycle Shop
- Paved Bike Trail
- Unpaved Bike Trail
- Equestrian Trail
- Proposed Trails

Safety and Trail Tips

Before you hit the trail, here are some suggestions so your explorations will be as carefree as possible.

- **"Wheels" on the right, "heels" on the left.** When using the bicycle trail, bicyclists (wheels) should stay on the right of the yellow line down the center of the trail, and hikers or joggers (heels) on the left. A wide dirt shoulder exists along most parts of the trail to alleviate congestion during busy hours.
- **Pull off onto the shoulder whenever you stop.** Bicyclists should also pass other bicyclists on the left and say "On your left" to indicate passing.
- **A speed limit of 15 mph exists on all parts of the Parkway.**
- **Bicyclists should stay on marked trails and off horse or hiking trails.**
- **Use common sense to avoid both poison oak and the infrequent mountain lion or rattlesnake.** In case of snake bite, the best treatment is to go immediately to the nearest hospital emergency room.
- **Emergency phones are placed at many locations on the lower 23 miles of the Parkway.** Public phones are available just off the trail. Both emergency and public phones are marked in the guide by symbols.
- **Respect your heritage by taking care of the Parkway.** Bag your own trash, and perhaps that of others not as considerate.
- **Collecting of plants or rocks is not permitted on the American River Parkway.**
- **The natural world is full of surprises.** No one should use any Parkway trails without assuming responsibility for any risks involved.

Every attempt has been made to make this guide as accurate as possible. We welcome your input. Please send suggestions or corrections to:

Biking and Hiking Guide
The American River Natural History Association
P.O. Box 241
Carmichael, CA 95609-0241
www.arnha.org

Horse Staging Areas

Public Day use fees: $10 for truck and trailer along the American River Parkway Discovery Park to Hazel Avenue.

AMERICAN RIVER PARKWAY NORTH BANK

Discovery Park. Easy access - east on Garden Hwy off Interstate 5. Look for Discovery Park sign on your right (at Natomas Park Drive intersection.) Large non-paved Equestrian staging area. Hitching rail and water and nearby bathroom. Equestrian trail follows Garden Hwy east under Park access road along south side of Bannon Slough. Area floods in winter. Beautiful ride in the summer. Flat terrain and shoes not necessary. Mosquito repellent comes in handy at times.

Cal Expo Area. There is access to the Parkway trails from the southernmost end of Ethan Way past Cal Expo. Minimal parking on pavement in cul de sac adjacent to Parkway.

William B. Pond Recreation Area. Easy access from east end of Arden Way in Carmichael. Non-paved staging area on your immediate right past the Entry Booth/Iron Ranger. Hitching rail, water trough and nearby bathrooom. Access the equestrian trail by crossing the paved road through the signed opening in post and cable fence just east of the Park entrance gates. Cross the Bike path with caution (near end of bridge) and (a) drop down to the trail along the river's edge to ride downstream. Areas of river rock and gravel footing. Some rolling terrain after passing stocked fishing pond with wheel-chair access. (b) if your horse is not easily spooked, ride across the bike/foot bridge, following the bike trail until signs direct to equestrian trails that skirt the south side of River Bend Park, and upstream.

Ancil Hoffman Park. Access from Fair Oaks Blvd. in Carmichael, east on Van Alstine. Turn left onto California Ave. and immediately right on Tarshes Dr. Shared paved parking on left immediately after Entry Booth/Iron Ranger. Arena close by.

Diverse but short trail loops around golf course, along a bluff, passes Effie Yeaw Nature Area and follows the American River through an oft-times busy picnic area.

Good footing, no rocks, small water crossing, and access to the river.

Sacramento Bar. Enter Parkway from Fair Oaks Blvd., south onto Pennsylvania Ave. (first street west of Sunrise). Staging area with hitching rail off pavement at far end of parking lot. Bathroom at far end of parking area (a) Pretty loop trail on north side of the river, and (b) Trails on south side of river can be accessed by crossing Jim's Bridge - at east end of parking lot. Can be an adventure sharing bridge with bicycles, inline skaters and fishers.

Sailor Bar. Enter Parkway from south end of Illinois Ave. Pretty trails to ride in the spring, can be hot in the summer. Bathroom near boat launch.

SOUTH AMERICAN RIVER

River Bend County Park. Non-paved staging area accessed from Rod Beaudry Drive off Folsom Blvd. Follow signs in the Parkway. Water trough, hitching rail and bathroom. a) Ride down-river - crossing pedestrian/bicycle bridge to William B. Pond Recreation Area, then drop down to river's edge directly after exiting the bridge. b) or ride upstream following marked trail. The terrain is flat, but in places the river bank has eroded and the equestrian trail is squeezed between the river and the bike trail. Summer weekends Hagan Park is congested, and a miniature train sometimes appears unexpectedly at the east end of that park. This could test if your mount is really spook-proof.

Lower Sunrise. Non-paved staging area. Access Parkway by turning east onto South Bridge Street from Sunrise Blvd. Turn left at T intersection after passing Entry Booth. Follow road under Sunrise Avenue Bridge and past paved parking area. Take a sharp right through post and cable opening into small, shady, non-paved staging area. Hitching rail, water trough and nearby bathroom. Intense use at times - watch for bicycles, rafts and fishers as you access the equestrian trail. a) Follow trail to river and proceed left on easy shaded trail with great footing. b) To travel upriver, proceed to your right traversing the approach to Jim's Bridge, then follow the equestrian trail past the bathrooms. c) It is also possible to access Sacramento Bar by crossing Jim's Bridge, and manoevering through the oft-times congested, paved areas. To exit Lower Sunrise staging area: If northbound on Sunrise Blvd., exit the Parkway by the route you entered. BUT if southbound on Sunrise, exit right out of staging area and follow paved road out of Parkway.

Hazel Ave. From south side of the river exit west off Hazel Ave. onto Gold Country Blvd., take second turn to right (not Nimbus Hatchery entrance), and continue to gravel parking area (past Region II Department of Fish and Game Headquarters). Hitching rail. Ride downstream on trail after traversing bicycle path. State Park trails can be accessed by traveling upstream and using multi-use covered bridge across Hazel Ave. (Not for the faint of heart!)

THE AMERICAN RIVER PARKWAY

The American River Parkway is abundant with ever–changing plants and creatures: towering oaks, colorful wildflowers, migrating chinook salmon, waterfowl and song birds, black–tailed deer, pipevine swallowtail butterflies, and even an occasional coyote, mountain lion or bald eagle. It is a work of art in progress, designed and redesigned by weather and seasons, wildlife, vegetation and human activity.

Storm waters and restoration projects resculpt banks and sweep away vegetation or even the trail. Non-native plants such as star thistle, Spanish broom, pampas grass and giant reed invade disturbed areas. Where plants such as chicory or wild fuchsia flourished for years, other vegetation is planted by breeze-scattered seeds, birds, squirrels or even humans. While acknowledging these changes, we have attempted to identify typical locations for plants and animals. The rest, and the best, is up to you.

So stop for a moment and hear the woodland chorus. Discover the tracks of the coyote and deer or follow a twisting trail to the lodge of the beaver. Listen to the not–so–dim voices and songs of those who came this way before us. The connections we share create within us a sense of belonging.

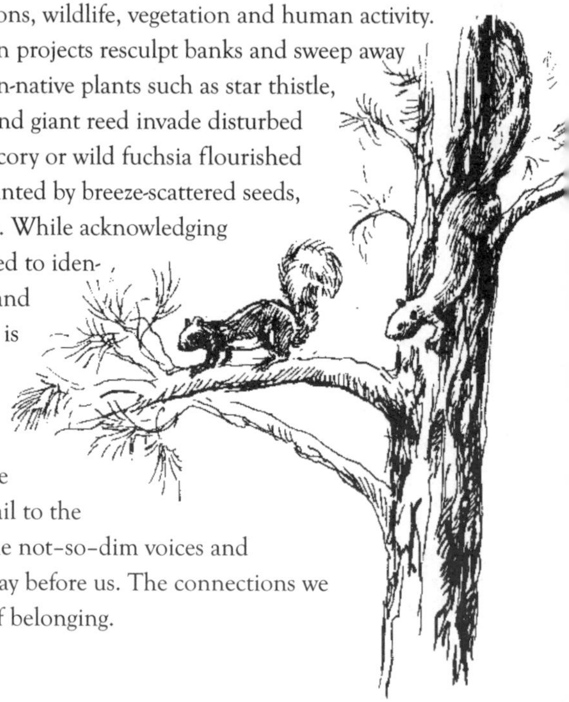

Observation hints

On your journey from the Sacramento River to Folsom Lake, you will pass through six distinct habitats and enough changes in elevation and climate that a type of plant found at one end of the Parkway may not be found at the other.

The plants and birds you will see may also vary depending on the time of year. Every season has unique opportunities for sightings. Winter is a good time for birding and viewing nests, animals and nature clues normally hidden from view. In spring, the woods come alive with mating calls, wildflowers and vibrant foliage.

As seasons change, other plants and creatures become unrecognizable from their former selves. In the spring butterflies emerge from their winter chrysalises, and dragonflies stretch new wings as they leave their watery world for the sky. By becoming familiar with Parkway flora and fauna, you will be able to track many "old friends" through their daily and seasonal rhythms.

And remember, the best sightings of wildlife are usually in the early morning or evening, or in the burst of activity after a rain. Rain hushes your approach and diminishes your scent. Learn to be patient. Your quiteness will often be rewarded with glimpses into another world.

Checklist

- **Bikers** — A bicycle lock is handy if you want to take walking side trips or stop at a nearby restaurant or shop. When using the trail, bring a bicycle tire tube kit, and wear a helmet.
- **Bikers and hikers** will find that although water fountains are strategically placed along the trail, it is a good idea to carry your own water bottle, especially in the summer. And don't forget to use sunscreen or a hat. If you want to see nature close up, binoculars and a magnifying glass can help open up a whole new world.
- **Discovering nature with children**—Take drinks and snacks and plan occasional rest stops. If you're doing a round trip, save enough energy for the return trip.
- **Nature and history guides** can help make your trip even more rewarding. *The Outdoor World of the Sacramento Region* and *Audubon's Checklist of Birds of the Sacramento Area* are two of the best nature guides for this area. Check the references for other resources.

American River Parkway

RANDY SMITH

The American River Bicycle Trail and the Sacramento skyline seen upriver from Howe Avenue Bridge

Welcoming trails invite you to take a closer look.

ROBIN DONELLY

RANDY SMITH

Bicycle bridge at Arden Bar

DAVID ROSEN/DUCKS UNLIMITED

DAVID ROSEN/DUCKS UNLIMITED

DAVID ROSEN/DUCKS UNLIMITED

Beaver plying smooth water in the evening.

HEADS UP! **Wild Turkey** introduced in the late 1800s–a familiar Parkway resident.

Show Your Support

for the American River Parkway!

American River Parkway Supporter jerseys are now available at the Effie Yeaw Nature Center.

100% of your purchase goes to support environmental education programs on the parkway.

Nature's Looking Glass. A great egret ...admiring himself, or looking for lunch?

DAVID ROSEN/DUCKS UNLIMITED

In spring, bright orange-red eggs are laid on the underside of **Dutchman's Pipe leaf.**

Eggs become **caterpillars** on leaves and seed pods.

DAVID ROSEN/DUCKS UNLIMITED

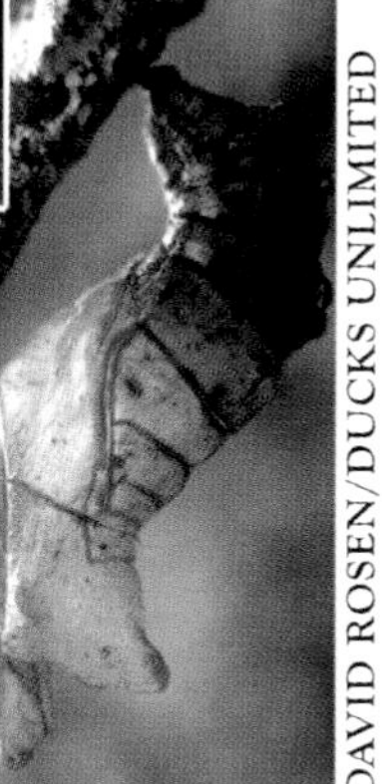

Pipevine Swallowtail Chrysalis– often found in protected places.

RANDY SMITH

Docent at the **Effie Yeaw Nature Center.**

DAVID ROSEN/DUCKS UNLIMITED

Arden Bar

Dawn at **Fair Oaks Bluff**

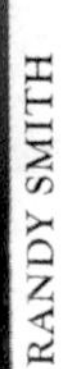

RANDY SMITH

The Jedediah Smith Memorial Bicycle Trail

The Jedediah Smith Memorial Bicycle Trail, named for the famous fur trapper and explorer, is a "*recycled*" concept. The first American River bicycle trail was built in 1896 by the Capital City Wheelmen, an early cycling club. The cinder path coursed along the south side of the American River from Sacramento to the town of Folsom. Bicycle enthusiasts and business people from both Sacramento and Folsom provided the financing for the trail. When farming traffic and rainy winters damaged the path, parts were replaced with decomposed granite. This improved surface allowed a new biking speed record of one hour and two minutes for the 20 miles between Sacramento and Folsom.

The arrival of the automobile caused bicycling to take a back seat. The bicycle trail disappeared until public support in the 1970s created the Jedediah Smith Memorial Bicycle Trail in the emerging American River Parkway. Today the average bicyclist can travel the almost 32-mile trail from Discovery Park to Beals Point in two to four hours, with a total climb of about 480 feet.

RANDY SMITH

Whether bicycling solely on the trail, or using it to commute to nearby destinations, the trail and your bicycle are a ticket to smog-free, calorie-burning transportation and adventure.

Discovery Park to Cal Expo

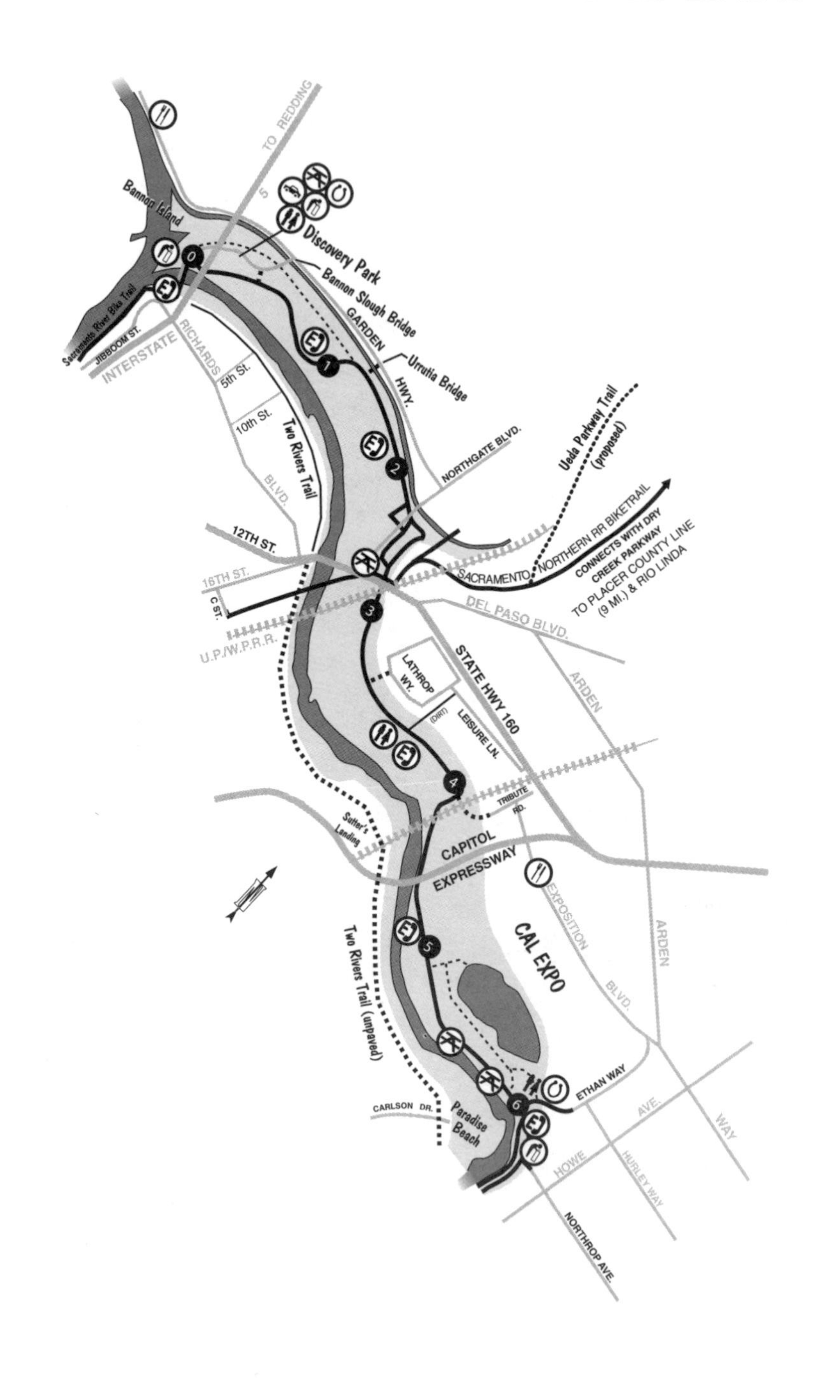

Discovery Park to Cal Expo

Miles 0-6

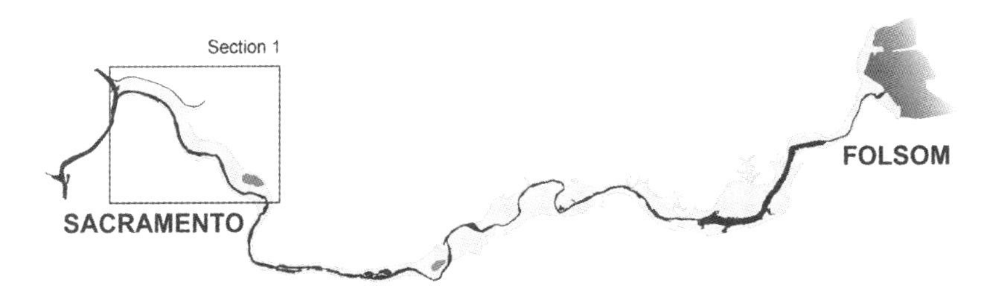

Discovery Park can be reached from the south by taking Richards Boulevard to the Jibboom Street Bridge and from the north by taking the Garden Highway to the Bannon Slough Bridge.

The six miles in this section of the Parkway introduce you to a unique area of the bicycle trail. The almost yearly flooding that inundates parts of these first few miles creates a swamp-like presence. You emerge at Cal Expo in a grasslands habitat–an elevation gain of about 15 feet at the high point near Mile 5. Along the way, you pass by the former locations of two Nisenan villages, Jedediah Smith's camp, John Sutter's landing, plus early bridge and ferry crossing sites. On the south side of the river, a paved section of the Two River Trails, opened in 2006, follows the river for a mile and two-thirds from Jibboom Street at Tiscornia Park at the confluence, to Highway 160 at N. 12th Street. The trail continues (unpaved as of 2011) for another four and a quarter miles from N. 12th Street to the "H" Street bridge, near CSU-Sacramento.

Begin your American River Parkway journey in Discovery Park. Under the shade of an old cottonwood tree near the Jibboom Street Bridge is the Jedediah Smith Bicycle Trail plaque followed by a sign marking the trail as far as Nimbus Dam. You can travel an additional nine miles beyond to Folsom Lake on the California State Park part of the bicycle trail. Equestrian and hiking trails stretch the length of the Parkway and often weave across the bicycle trail.

Jedediah Smith, a bible–toting beaver trapper, was the first American explorer to stand at the confluence of the American and Sacramento Rivers. Leading a party of trappers from the Rocky Mountains, he reached the fur–rich American in April 1827. Smith was impressed with the untamed river's turbulence and his encounters with the area's grizzly bears, but it was the "wildness" of the native population living along its banks that caused him to name it the "wild river."

Discovery Park's 385 acres boast boat launching facilities, picnic areas, volleyball courts, archery ranges, an equestrian staging area, a trail, and good fishing. Early settlers would claim that during salmon runs there were so many fish you could walk on their backs to cross the river, and so many birds and elk you just had to pull out your gun and shoot.

Ⓢ
Confluence

Before you continue on the bicycle trail, take a few minutes to travel toward the point which juts into the Sacramento River. Picnic tables make this area a welcome place for a snack. Off the point, anglers catch striped bass and catfish, and in the fall, salmon and steelhead swimming toward their American River spawning grounds. Check out the old cottonwood tree that stands nearby. Huge knots contort this ancient tree, and a hole at the base of its trunk is a good home for animals.

Large **Fremont cottonwoods** shade the bicycle trail. These distinctive trees can grow to 90 feet tall and live more than a hundred years. In the spring cottonwoods form soft cottony seeds and heart-shaped leaves which rustle in even a light breeze. Our local cottonwood is named after John Fremont who visited this area with Kit Carson. Explorers like Fremont and later settlers looked for cottonwoods because they meant the welcome presence of water and shade. The sweet inner bark was also food for their horses.

Travel under the Jibboom Street Bridge. California sycamore trees along the trail have been hollowed out by fire, although their whitish bark retains a beautiful majesty. Hollowed–out trees survive because it is the inner layer of bark that carries life in the tree.

The **Mile 0** marker is just before the I–5 overpass. Enter an area with grapevines draping large cottonwoods, square–stemmed blue vervain, blackberries, sweet fennel, chicory, seasonal wild flowers, and box elders. California box elder trees do well along river and stream banks where they may grow to 50 feet high. Look for their distinctive compound leaf made up of three leaflets. V–shaped winged seeds hang from the limbs even in winter.

The old channel of the American River once ran south from this area. In 1868 it was filled in, eliminating one of the river's broad curves where flood water poured into the downtown area. Parts of Discovery Park still flood after heavy winter or spring rains.

The two trails heading north after the kiosk lead to the **Discovery Park Nature Trail, Bannon Island** and the **Sacramento River Bicycle Trail**. The nature hiking trail can be reached on the south side of the Bannon Slough Bridge. Bannon Island and an assortment of riverfront restaurants are reached by crossing the Bannon Slough Bridge and taking a left on the Sacramento River Bicycle Trail, along the southern edge of the Garden Highway.

Ⓢ

Bannon Island

Bannon Island, *on the northwestern edge of Discovery Park, is a half–mile west of the Bannon Slough Bridge. During rainy seasons, access to the island's hiking trails is cut off by Bannon Slough.*

Bannon Island is one of the last valley oak savannahs left in the Sacramento Valley. Plants such as prickly lettuce, curly dock, poison oak, blackberry, Indian hemp and rare grasses lie at its heart. A colony of threatened valley elderberry longhorn beetles find refuge in the island's elderberry trees. Hawks soar above a giant valley oak which is about 250 years old. Its acorns have sprouted into the young oak forest nearby.

Traveling east on the bicycle trail, you pass the site of the **Nisenan village of Pujune**. Nearly 500 people lived here until the 1830s. Pujune was a village of dome-shaped willow and tule houses built on a mound to protect against flooding.

Forty Nisenan archeological sites have been recorded along the Lower American River.

A public archery range begins on the north side of the trail just before **Mile 0.5**. Nisenan made their arrows from straight shoots of willow, elderberry, alder, or buckeye. You will be able to find many of these trees as you enter into the swamp-like riparian habitat up the trail.

Willows are erect shrubs or trees with slender, pointed leaves and gray stems with red-tipped new growth. Before they leaf out in the spring, the catkins or pussy willows appear on bare branches. Nisenan also used willow to make homes, granaries, traps and baskets. They burned gray willow stands to enhance the growth of multiple sprouts of the needed size. The Nisenan also peeled and chewed willow for toothaches. Tea made from boiled bark was given for fevers. The salicin in willow bark is the active ingredient in aspirin.

By **Mile 0.75** plants such as sweet fennel have replaced the forest, and great clumps of blackberry bushes mound in the field north of the trail, providing good cover for wildlife.

MILE 1

Near the **Mile 1** marker is a colorful succession of plants. In the spring, wet years help produce a tall variety of perennial pepper grass (whitetop). As summer progresses, a colorful display of brilliant yellow sunflowers and curly dock takes over. Curly dock can grow to four feet high and is green in spring and reddish-brown in summer and fall. Curly dock's young tender leaves make a good addition to a salad, soup or stew.

The trail continues north toward Bannon Slough, an important backwater drainage tributary and wetlands habitat. Then it swings east to parallel privately owned property to the south.

At the stop sign at **Mile 1.25, Urrutia Bridge** provides access to the Garden Highway. The nature hiking trail also meets with the bicycle trail here. On the river side of the bike trail are an old house and a nearby sand and topsoil pit that has become a large pond. For many years, the Urrutia family has been mining soils at this 122-acre site. This parcel and the adjoining Boy Scout camp and trailer park just upriver are some of the few areas between the river and the bike trail that are not a part of the Parkway.

Stay right as the bicycle trail divides at **Mile 1.8**.

At **Mile 2** alder and non-native silver maple trees grace the median strip between the trails. In summer look for the **common sunflower (*mirasol*)**. Their Spanish name means "looks at the sun" because their yellow heads follow the sun each day. These tall flowers are very attractive to monarch butterflies and furnish seeds for birds late into the summer. Nisenan ground sunflower seeds into a meal and used the oil for cooking and dressing hair.

A short distance up the trail is the access to **Northgate Boulevard**, so named because it served as the important northern gate to early travelers between Sacramento and Marysville, Auburn, and the gold fields on the north side of the American River. The next eight miles of the trail are in an area once known as **Rancho Del Paso**, a 44,000 acre Mexican land grant given to Captain Eliab Grimes in 1844.

Rancho Del Paso

Eliab Grimes, a Honolulu merchant, came to San Francisco in 1839. In 1844 the Mexican governor granted him 44,000 acres of rich lands adjoining Sutter's New Helvetia. By 1862, the ranch was owned by James Ben Ali Haggin and Lloyd Tevis and entered its heyday, becoming famous for the breeding of thoroughbred horses. In 1885, Haggin horses won the modern equivalent of more than $3,000,000 in purse money, the largest amount ever won in one season by a single stable. The following year Haggin's Ben Ali won the Kentucky Derby.

In 1909 the aging horseman sold the Rancho to an eastern land company. They advertised the area as a subdivision of high-class villa homesites with a wandering creek and stately oaks, minutes from Sacramento by way of three distinct rail lines.Today glimpses of Rancho Del Paso's former glory live on in local place names reminding us of Haggin, Ben Ali and his famous thoroughbreds.

Just after Northgate, look for **button bush** shrubs (also known as button willow because of its willow-like leaves) on the north side of the trail. The round blossom clusters of this shrub give the plant its name and are especially attractive to butterflies.

A short alternate route skirts the site of a Sacramento Area Flood Control Agency (SAFCA) wetlands habitat restoration project. The man-made backwaters created when soil is "borrowed" and placed to build up levees in developed areas are important habitat enhancements. The floods of 1986, 1995, and 1997 have also made it clear that rivers, one of the most dynamic systems in nature, need room to roam beyond the corsets of the levees. This particular area contains water coming down Steelhead Creek.

Near Mile **2.4** the trail turns south at the levee. Bannon Slough continues north, draining waters from the Natomas East Main Drain, including Dry Creek and **Arcade Creek**.

Arcade Creek and the "Big Four"

During the creation of the Central Pacific Railroad in the 1860s, the "Big Four" (Huntington, Stanford, Crocker and Hopkins) maintained that since the soil seemed brown on the west side of Arcade Creek and red on the east, the red–soiled foothills began just east of the creek. Though unsubstantiated, this finding allowed the Central Pacific to get paid the foothill rate of $48,000 per mile of laid track, three times the flatland rate. Pressed for supply routes for the Civil War and western expansion, President Lincoln approved the railroad grant. The "Big Four" were thereafter known as "men who could move mountains."

As you continue up river, another seasonal marsh borders the trail, formed when soil was excavated to build the levee.

Near **Mile 2.6** watch for runners, hikers and bicyclists on top of the levee. They are enjoying the **Sacramento Northern Railroad** (SNRR) easement. Part of the old railroad bed has become the SNRR/Rio Linda Bike Trail.

Sacramento Northern Railroad Bike Trail

*Just after **Mile 2.6**, west of the stop sign at Del Paso Boulevard, travel north on the 9-mile **SNRR Bike Trail.** The trail leads from downtown Sacramento, meets with the Jedediah Smith Memorial Trail here, and continues to M Street in Rio Linda. The parkway the Natomas drainage canal to the Placer County line.*

Near **Mile 2.7** is the stop sign at **Del Paso Boulevard.** This busy street was another main thoroughfare carrying miners and Sacramentans to towns north. Look north where the road intersects the levee to see the emergency flood gates. These gates are closed if water floods this area.

Pink Cadillac

A short side trip down Del Paso Boulevard to the river ends at a mobile home park where parts of the Clint Eastwood movie, Pink Cadillac, were filmed. A quaint old residence is now used as an office. West of the trailer park is Camp Pollack, the Boy Scout camp, complete with riverside clubhouse.

After crossing Del Paso Boulevard, a trail spur leads south to the old **Sacramento Northern Railroad/18th Street Bicycle Bridge** into Sacramento. During flooding in the winter or spring, use this access to downtown because the bicycle trail to the Jibboom Street Bridge may be under water.

Views from the Bridge

Take the trail spur toward the river. Between the bicycle bridge and the 12th Street Highway Bridge is the site of Ueda Park.

Near here was ***Jedediah Smith's 1828 campsite.*** *His diary reported two trappers shot two Indians found by the camp's traps. Not too surprisingly, the whole tribe fled when Smith's party reached Pujune two miles west. One young girl died of fright causing a distraught and remorseful Smith to cover her body with presents.*

Proceed toward the river and onto the SNRR Bridge, built near the turn of the century. In the early 1900s, this iron bridge was also used by the Northern Electric Railroad when Sacramento boasted both efficient cable cars and electric railways.

Near where Highway 160 crosses the river is the site of ***Lisle's Ferry and Lisle's Bridge*** *which connected to Northgate and Del Paso roads. During the 1850s and 1860s Lisle's bridge washed out with each large flood, allowing steamships to make their way upriver. When the 80-foot steamer Daisy went upriver in 1882, it had to be run aground and winched around the bridge to the other side. In 1888, the bridge was replaced by the 12th Street Bridge.*

SACRAMENTO HISTORY AND SCIENCE ARCHIVES

Bridge tolls encouraged thrifty travelers to ford the river when it was low.

To the east is the Western Pacific Railroad Bridge, now used by Union Pacific. Notice that the railroad bridge footings are completely out of the water at most times of the year. When the bridge was built, the river bed was higher than it is now. Lack of silt and the resultant downcutting by clear water has caused a drop in the riverbed.

Retrace your route back to the Jedediah Smith Bicycle trail unless you are planning to loop into downtown Sacramento.

As you near **Mile 2.8**, cross under the Highway 160 overpasses and the Western Pacific/Union Pacific Railway Trestle. You are leaving the Discovery Park section of the Parkway and entering the area known as **Woodlake** which extends for about a mile to the old Central Pacific Railroad tracks.

MILE 3

The trail becomes a corridor created by the levee on one side and a riparian wetlands area on the other. Tenacious grapevines hang from huge cottonwoods over an understory of willow trees and poison oak. Vegetation in these lowland areas of the Parkway is well adapted to periodic flooding. Flooding allows plants like these to receive an annual subsidy of leaves and nutrient–rich goop from upriver and gives many seeds the bath they need to germinate.

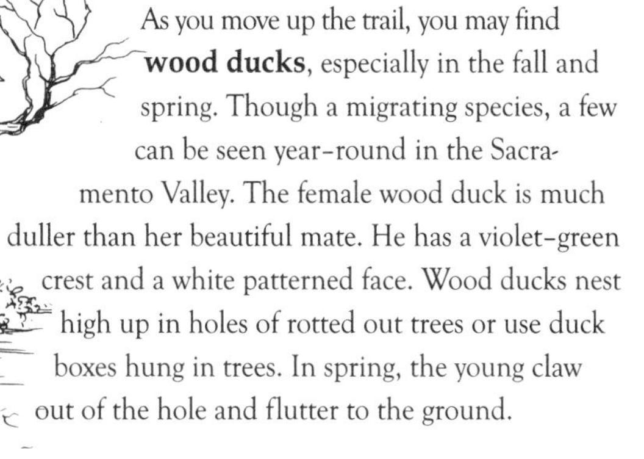

As you move up the trail, you may find **wood ducks**, especially in the fall and spring. Though a migrating species, a few can be seen year–round in the Sacramento Valley. The female wood duck is much duller than her beautiful mate. He has a violet–green crest and a white patterned face. Wood ducks nest high up in holes of rotted out trees or use duck boxes hung in trees. In spring, the young claw out of the hole and flutter to the ground.

As you approach **Mile 3.2**, an access trail leads to **Lathrop Way**. From the levee you can look toward the walnut trees to the northwest where the Nisenan villagers of nearby **Sekumne (Sek)** foraged for nuts in the fall. The descriptive Nisenan language reflects important aspects of their lives. Months were called…"ripe seed month, birds fly north, smaller month, leaves on tree, and flower month." (Orr, *Rivers of the West*)

By **Mile 3.3** the cottonwood trees thin out. In the fall, non-native silver maple trees catch your attention with their colorful autumn display. Brown, winged seed pods hang on their bare branches into the winter. Beyond the marsh, the cultivated fields with the radio station towers in the distance are destined to be another SAFCA wetlands area. Mallard ducks often dabble for food in shallows here. Many dabblers are good at finding food both on and off the water. Dabblers must strain many gallons of water through serrations in their long flat bills to obtain the seeds and the tiny plants and animals which make up much of their diet.

The leaves of arrowhead and water plantain rise from marshy areas. In summer, small white flowers form. Arrowhead is also known as tule potato because its tubers were used for food and were cultivated by early Chinese miners in the Sacramento area.

Near **Mile 3.6** big runoff drainage pipes empty into the marsh.

Mile 3.7 is at the intersection of the trail with the dirt levee road connecting to **Leisure Lane** at the Radisson Hotel.

By **Mile 3.9** part of an old washed-out bicycle trail branches toward the marsh. Near this old bicycle trail are beaver-gnawed cottonwoods and willows. Since a tree totally girdled by a beaver dies, some of the cottonwood trees in this area have protective metal screens around their bases.

Take a look at the tule plants growing along the marsh edge here. **Common tules** are tall leafless perennials which you can see throughout the year. In summer, reddish-brown to straw-colored flowers emerge at the top of the stalklike stem. Tules' hard-coated seeds, tender stems and roots nourish waterfowl and shore birds. Dense stands provide nesting sites and shelter for marsh wrens and blackbirds as well as waterfowl. Nisenan used tules to make small boats and to weave mats and skirts. They twisted it into cordage, thatched their summer houses and lined their granaries. They also gathered the roots and ate them raw or cooked and sometimes made them into a nutritious flour.

Nightshade, which averages two feet high and resembles a dainty version of its relative, the tomato plant, can sometimes be found here in spring and summer. White or lavender flowers become shiny black berries that are considered poisonous. It is said that the common name, nightshade, originated because in the shade of night, witches brewed the juice of Belladonna (beautiful lady). Nightshade was used by Spanish maidens to dilate their eyes in order to enhance their beauty.

As you near **Mile 4** the trail makes a turn toward the river at the old **Central Pacific** railroad tracks. For the next two-tenths of a mile you will be paralleling the tracks that led across a growing nation and shortened the transcontinental journey which once took many dangerous months into one lasting a matter of days.

At **Mile 4.1** a bicycle and pedestrian railroad underpass leads to the **Tribute Road/Cal Expo** access. To reach restaurants, travel out Tribute Road and go east on Exposition Boulevard.

For an historic side trip do not go under the trestle but continue straight on the old bke trail. This hiking side trip intercepts the bicycle trail in a mile.

River of Change

Travel by foot across the equestrian trail toward the river's edge. The hill across the river rests on top of the southern arc of the old river channel, filled in 1868. The area later served as the city dump until 1994. It is now being converted to ***Sutter's Landing Park,*** *a 173–acre "urban retreat," to commemorate where* ***John Sutter*** *landed with his small group of Hawaiians and Europeans to found "New Helvetia" on August 12, 1839.*

After Sutter was settled on shore, departing crew members anxious to return to Yerba Buena (San Francisco) were given a roaring cannon fire salute. The cannon impressed the Nisenan and discouraged them from resisting Sutter. A few whites and the ten Hawaiians remained. The Hawaiian huts they built at the landing site are, of course, long gone. The restored Sutter's Fort at 27th and L Streets is a reminder that while many Americans were slowly pushing the frontier westward from Missouri, Sutter grabbed an immense empire by slipping in the backdoor from the Pacific.

Occasionally a freight train grinds its way across the river on the railroad bridge built in 1912. The first bridge to cross here was built in 1863 for the Central Pacific Railroad and was the longest bridge and trestle between Sacramento and Promontory, Utah. At low water, old bridge foundations can be seen on the upriver side of the existing bridge.

Listen for the call of the Nuttall's woodpecker as it makes its way among the willow, walnut, cottonwood and elderberry, or see raccoon and beaver tracks in the sandy soil along the river bank. The grapevines and brambles contribute to the sense that this area is similiar to the riparian forests known to the Nisenan. A look at the Sacramento skyline just beyond the river offers a contrasting image of today's world.

A quarter mile up the trail near the freeway a wetland has some mysteriously shaped cottonwood stumps. When this depression is dry, it appears that these trees were attacked by

SACRAMENTO HISTORY AND SCIENCE ARCHIVES

Getting across the river was no easy job. This Southern Pacific locomotive on an old American River trestle was one of several trains which ended up in the river.

flying beavers. You're looking at evidence of beaver activity when the swamp was at its high wintertime water level. ***Beavers*** *are constantly gnawing on twigs and the bark of trees. While they feed, their continuously growing front teeth are worn down. Watch for these shy nocturnal creatures at dusk and in the early morning in Parkway wetlands, or along stretches of quiet river. A slap of their broad tail on the water may alert you to their presence.*

Beavers' thick brown fur was once so valuable they were almost totally exterminated in our area. During a fashion craze for men's dress hats made of beaver in the 1800s, beaver furs sold for hundreds of dollars each. Most beavers found along the American River build no dams but burrow into the bank or construct their twiggy homes at the water's edge.

By the early 1850s the Upper (Sinclair) Ferry crossed the river here at the site of an old river ford. The fees at the Upper Ferry were $1.50 a person on foot, $4 a person and horse by day, and $8 by night. Since the men courting the three girls living at Norris Ranch found it beneath their dignity to arrive for their evening visits on foot, their ferry bill was $16 each, a small fortune by those days' standards.

Upper Ferry also brought passengers to the famous gardens of A. P. Smith, just across the river. Until the great floods of 1862, Smith's Gardens, more than two miles of white shelled paths through 90 acres of fruit trees, camellias, roses, and grape and berry vines, was an attractive outing for early Sacramentans. Continue your outing up the trail.

Passing under the railroad trestle, you are now entering the **Cal Expo Area**, which extends from here to the Ethan Way exit upriver. Though entirely within the American River Parkway, the floodplain here is under the jurisdiction of the Cal Expo Board of Directors. The Parks Department manages the Cal Expo flood plain with a special management agreement. The trail meanders through a field of sweet fennel, grapes and elderberry.

From May to August, feathery sweet fennel's yellow flowers appear in umbels, like upside-down umbrellas. Toward fall they become delicious seeds clustering on the tall, dry stalks. Their licorice taste makes them popular in soups, stews, cakes and cookies. In California's Spanish days, stalks of sweet fennel were spread on the floor of churches to give off a pleasant licorice odor when bruised by the feet of the congregation.

Pond and Meadow

Go through the underpass for a spring side trip which often provides a look at the mating and nesting behavior of ***red-winged blackbirds.*** *Beginning in late March these gregarious birds converge at the pond on the other side of the trestle. The males strut around with puffed up red shoulder patches which look like epaulets. The camouflaged dull brown–colored female has the job of egg incubation in nests attached to upright stems of water plants or branches of small trees.*

In the spring, blue dick and brodiaeas can be found in the grassy meadow here. They have leaves resembling grass and grow from the root. Blue dick has small purple–blue flowers clustered close together. The brodiaea, Ithuriel's Spear, has a loosely bunched larger cluster of violet–blue flowers. Harvest brodiaea blooms later, is more purple, and has fewer flowers. Nisenan used a sharp stick to dig these and other edible corms, and thus were sometimes called "Diggers" by white settlers. They would take the largest corm for roasting and replant the smaller corms in loosened soil.

The purple–blue splash of color you see from June to October along the trail is chicory. Early Egyptians roasted chicory roots on hot stones, or like the Greeks, used it as a salad herb.

Today, along the Parkway, Sacramentans can enjoy seeing hundreds of species of the 7,000 types of wildflowers that can be found in California, as well as hundreds of species of weeds. As you move up the trail for the next mile, keep in mind that even waste areas may be full of interest, value, and hidden connections.

Weeds?

According to Ralph Waldo Emerson, "A weed is a plant whose virtues have not yet been discovered." The dandelion found in moist, sunny areas in the Parkway is a hardy plant that has saved people from starvation and is relished in salads or made into wine. ***Common purslane,*** *a fleshy, red-stemmed garden vegetable, is prized in Europe and China but is considered a weed here. It has thick, wedge–shaped leaves and small yellow flowers that open when the sun shines. The tender ends can be used in salads or as a boiled green. Though it is much harder to find redemption in the invasive star thistle, bees do make honey from its nectar, gold finches eat the seeds, and a prickly cover is provided for a wide variety of animals.*

Nearing **Mile 5** a familiar Parkway plant, the Mexican tea, can sometimes be found. Pungent and hairy-stemmed, it grows in clumps to three feet high and has tiny green ball-like flowers and narrow toothed leaves. Early Spanish Californians boiled the leaves, making a tea to relieve upset stomachs.

The 86-acre Bushy Lake Nature Preserve to the north is an important habitat for plants and wildlife. Among the trees is **Bushy Lake**. The lake, shown on some of the first maps of the area, was once filled by recurrent high water from the river. Now it is largely filled by pumps at Cal Expo. Some of the nearby trails and service roads across this floodplain provide access.

In the distance, north of the trail is the Cal Expo water tower, and to the east the Cal Expo horse racing track. River water is used for canals, lakes, and fountains at the 630–acre Cal Expo site, now the home of the state fair. Sacramento has been the **California State Fair's** permanent site since 1861. This Cal Expo site has been used since 1968. The fair is an eighteen-day event, beginning in mid–July. Biking to attend the fair eliminates the hassle of parking.

You can often see raptors such as kites, red-tailed hawks, northern harriers and kestrels here. Their eyesight is much better than humans, making it easier for them to spot their dinner of mice, rabbits, ground squirrels, insects, and snakes. Unlike other birds, predator's eyes have evolved to become closer together so that they can determine the distance to their prey.

See whether you can spot white-tailed kites gliding over the Bushy Lake nature preserve. Kites look similiar to gulls but sport black shoulder marking and prefer marshes and open fields like these. Watch them hover suspended above the field before they sink to the ground to seize their prey of mice and voles. Having made a comeback under species protection laws, kites can also be seen in communal roosts on the Parkway.

Nearing **Mile 5.2** you can see where an arson fire in 1994 destroyed dozens of cottonwood trees and the riparian undergrowth. Cottonwoods are especially susceptible to damage because fire funnels up their highly flammable, deeply grooved bark. **Evening primrose** has taken advantage of the ash–enriched soil here. Avoiding the sun's harsh rays, evening primroses' butter–yellow flowers open rapidly in the evening and wither by mid–morning. They are pollinated by a night–flying sphinx moth as big as a hummingbird. The oil of one variety of primrose is one of the world's richest sources of natural, unsaturated, fatty acids.

At the bend in the trail is giant reed (false bamboo), a fast–growing invader which also thrived after the fire. This unwelcome plant may reach 20 feet in height and has tough perennial roots.

Near **Mile 5.5 blue elderberry** shrubs flourish. From April through July, tiny whitish–yellow elderberry blossoms grow in flat-topped clusters. As summer progresses, the blossoms become small purplish–blue berries. Nisenan found many uses for elderberry, which they called *K'a K'am* (tree of music). The wood was made into fire drills, arrows, flutes, whistles and clapper sticks for music making.

Blue elderberry shrubs provide shelter for many birds and the valley elderberry longhorn beetle, a species protected under U.S. law. Since more than 90% of California stream and riverside woodlands have been destroyed, the elderberry shrubs required by the beetles for food and egg laying are becoming more rare. Campaigns to save any of California's more than 100 threatened and endangered species are also efforts to save the habitat in which they live.

Near **Mile 5.6** a landmark black walnut tree graces the north side of the trail. These heavy–limbed trees have deeply furrowed bark, compound leaves, and a female flower which becomes a delicious walnut hidden inside a tough, brown husk. The Nisenan used walnuts for food and dyes.

Large herds of antelope, elk and deer once roamed these plains. In the 1840s, after **John Sinclair** set up Rancho Del Paso for Eliab Grimes, cattle trod upon this land. Near here, Sinclair would treat his guests to pieces of meat and game skewered and dripping over a fire and was "...a talented man and capital company where grog and cards were stirring." (John Yates, Master of Sutter's schooner *Sacramento*.)

A beautiful gamebird which had not yet made it here from China during Sinclair's era is the ring–necked **pheasant**. The cock has a green head with a neck circled in white. The modest brown of the female suits her well for her role of hatching her young in grass-lined nests built on the ground. Fast runners and unwilling fliers, pheasants, when startled, often rise straight up like a helicopter before assuming an appropriate course. Listen for their loud "kork–kok" call as you venture up the trail.

Near **Mile 5.8** picnic tables are shaded by a stand of walnut trees. Across the river is **Paradise Beach**. A popular beach since the 1880s, in 1950 it was the first piece of land purchased for the new American River Parkway.

The trail now becomes winding and is lined with willows. Sandbar willow is one of the first trees to grow in newly created sandbars or floodplains. This pioneer tree guards against erosion and helps ready the soil for other trees. Since trees have different water and soil requirements, the type of tree in an area can tell you about the soils and water availabilty.

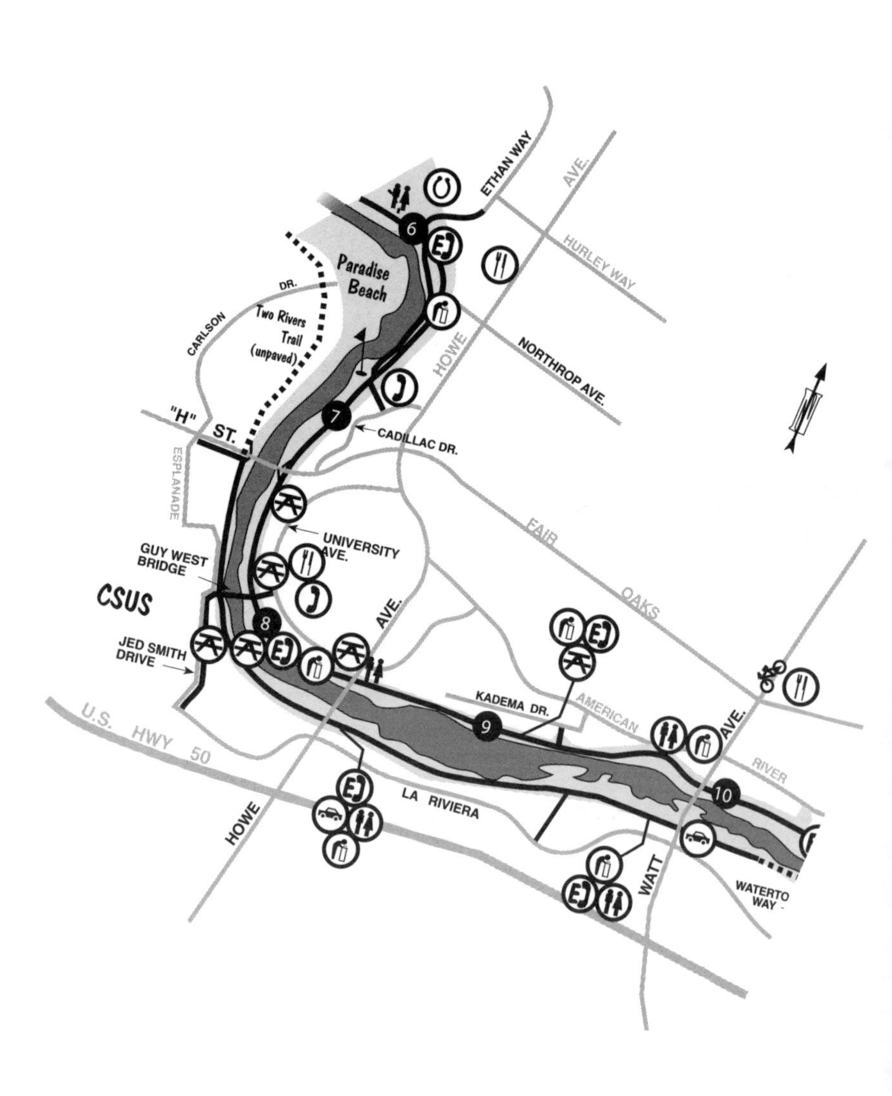
ETHAN WAY
AVE.
HURLEY WAY
Paradise Beach
DR.
CARLSON
Two Rivers Trail (unpaved)
HOWE
NORTHROP AVE.
"H" ST.
CADILLAC DR.
ESPLANADE
FAIR
UNIVERSITY AVE.
GUY WEST BRIDGE
OAKS
CSUS
AVE.
JED SMITH DRIVE
KADEMA DR.
AMERICAN
U.S. HWY 50
AVE.
RIVER
LA RIVIERA
HOWE
WATT
WATERTO WAY

CAL EXPO TO WATT AVENUE

Miles 6-10

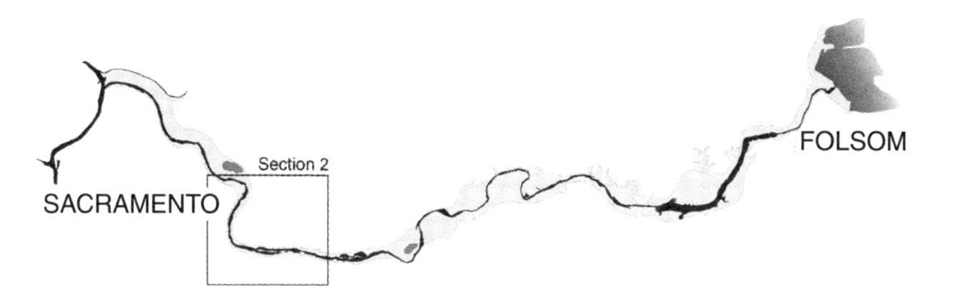

At **Mile 6** is an access trail between the **Bushy Lake/Cal Expo** Area and **Ethan Way**. Public parking is on Ethan Way.

The four miles of bicycle trail in this section will take you by the campus of California State University Sacramento, John Fremont and Kit Carson's campsite and historic town and Nisenan village sites. Vegetation, mammals and birds make good use of this narrow riparian strip. The equestrian trail and two alternative bicycle trails take advantage of the natural and cultural history of this area. One trail runs near the route of the Pony Express and the Capital City Wheelmen's path of 100 years ago.

A plaque near the kiosk marks the **U.S. Constitution Grove**, one of the many projects of the Sacramento Tree Foundation.

Farther east up the trail is the **Campus Commons Area** which continues to Howe Avenue Bridge. This area is a mixture of riparian vegetation and grass-lands wedged between the river and levee.

The brick flood control facility after **Mile 6.1** is one of several pumping stations on the Parkway. When the river or sloughs are high enough to flow into

In 1955, flood waters spread out on both sides of H Street Bridge, covering the hop fields where Campus Commons now stands.

SACRAMENTO HISTORY AND SCIENCE ARCHIVES

this channel, one by one the pumps are triggered to keep water from inundating the residential and business areas.

Creeks and Sloughs

It is worth the short climb to the top of the levee here. You can see the huge drainage collection area where the cemented channels of **Chicken Ranch and Strong Ranch Sloughs** *meet the Parkway. Many creeks and sloughs were "channelized" just as these sloughs were when land along the river was developed. When creeks are left in their natural state they reflect an intricate ecosystem which supports a variety of plant and animal life. Also, natural streams with surrounding vegetation serve to filter urban runoff and allow recharging of underlying water tables.*

Next to the pumping station is the old **Arden sewage treatment facility**. Treated sewage is no longer being dumped into the American River, though you can still see remnants of old facilities like this one along the Parkway. Now a lifting station, this facility elevates sewage so gravity will carry it through pipes under the river to the regional wastewater treatment plant in the Freeport/Elk Grove area.

At the wooden-railed overpass near **Mile 6.2, Chicken and Strong Ranch Sloughs** flow to the river. After the overpass, a two-thirds mile loop of the bike trail damaged in the flood of 1986 runs toward the river.

Riparian Loop

Travel toward the river on this riparian loop. This trail offers solitude, shade, restful river views and a more natural riverine habitat. The downed trees or snags you will see are an important part of nature's cycle. Organisms of many kinds unlock the stored nutrients in trees and make them available to other creatures essential to forest food chains. Meanwhile, the tree provides food and shelter–a veritable habitat hotel–for cavity–nesters. Eventually, the tree's soft organic matter slows erosion and becomes a moist, nutrient–rich mulch in which seedlings root. Return to the main trail near Mile 6.8 at the eastern edge of the Campus Commons Golf Course.

Continuing on the main trail, notice how the vetches, curly dock, grapevines and box elder trees thin out as you enter a walnut forest. Toxins in the decomposing walnut husks prevent other plants from growing in places where the nuts fall. In autumn, walnuts covering the ground here make a feast for magpies and crows. Crows are related to jays, magpies and ravens, which are among the most intelligent of birds. They were respected by the Nisenan for their intelligence and the beauty of their black feathers which were woven into feather robes and shamans' caps.

Near **Mile 6.4**, you may take the nearby **Northrop Avenue** access ramp or staircase a couple of short blocks to restaurants on Howe Avenue and Enterprise Drive. A drinking fountain is under an old black walnut tree. Opposite the drinking fountain, a hiking trail leads into a natural and secluded area.

As you move up the trail, deer, birds, rabbits, mice, and perhaps an intriguing, but seldom seen, critter known as a ringtail, or "miner's cat," make use of shelter provided by twining leaves. The **ringtail** is an efficient night hunter for small mammals, insects, fruit, and berries. Early settlers befriended these shy critters to curb the mice population.

Messy–looking magpie nests have roofs and can often be seen in the tops of the trees, especially during the winter when the limbs are bare of leaves. Yellow-billed magpies, found only in the Central Valley and some of the coastal valleys, are one of the Parkway's most familiar birds. The Sierra makes an effective barrier, separating this species from its black–billed relative. Their distinct white and black markings, yellow bill and noisy habits make them hard to miss. Gregarious and intelligent, they perform useful scavenging jobs in fields, backyards, and along city streets.

At **Mile 6.5** is a junction with the equestrian trail. Oak and cottonwood trees offer a welcome contrast to the starkness of the powerlines, levee, and apartment buildings along the north side of the trail.

In summer, look for **western kingbirds** in areas like this. Slightly smaller than a robin, this trim bird has a yellow–bellied gray body. When it leaves a perch to snap up insects, you can see a white outline on its black tail feathers. The male kingbird is known for his loud tyrannical warning screech and aggressive behavior. If a small predator ignores the warning and ventures too close to his mate's nest, it could be attacked or even killed. Upon acquiring adult plumage, however, the once carefully-tended young are ousted from the nest.

Migratory Life Rafts

Kingbirds herald the beginning of summer and are one of dozens of migratory species using the American River Parkway for a prolonged sojourn or a resting and refueling stop. In the fall and winter, songbirds like the yellow-rumped warbler and white-crowned sparrow and waterfowl like the common goldeneye find refuge here.

As primary habitat is damaged, the preservation of flyways in–between, such as the American River Parkway, become all the more important.

Near **Mile 6.8**, just west of the **Campus Commons Golf Course**, is a picnic table and junction where the riparian bike trail loop joins the main trail. Built in 1972, the golf course leases land from the County.

MILE

Mile 7 finds you traversing between the course and the levee. Non-native, low–growing crab and bermuda grasses are used on levee banks because they

grow low enough to allow visual inspection of the levee and are not a fire hazard. A hearty native alternative grass, and one which out-competes yellow star thistle, is creeping wild rye.

Pass over the storm drain at **Mile 7.1**. Wild radish is a common plant along the trail from late winter to late summer. These multibranched weeds are a colorful potpourri of white, yellow, pink, and lavender four-petaled flowers.

At **Mile 7.25** is **H Street Bridge**, built by the county in 1932. The access, located on the upriver side of the bridge, takes you to Fair Oaks Boulevard or over the bridge to H Street (where you can connect with a bicycle trail on the south side of the river). The fertile area on both sides of the river was once covered with hop fields.

In the 1930s, this giant slide created a big splash near H Street Bridge

SACRAMENTO HISTORY AND SCIENCE ARCHIVES

Across the river in 1852, the supply town of **Hoboken** (and in 1862, **Mitchville**), bloomed for a couple months during flooding which severed Sacramento's rail and roads connection to the mines. To reach these towns, steamboats bearing supplies from Sacramento struggled past washed-out bridges on their trips up the swollen river. After 1862, Sacramento's soggy inhabitants straightened the river bends above the city, so high waters would not isolate the city again.

Immediately after the bridge is a shady picnic table and resting place near black locust trees. These large trees have deeply furrowed grey bark and distinctive oval-shaped leaflets. In the winter, brown seed pods hang from the tree. In the spring the fragrance of the tree's white flowers help you understand why they were imported by early settlers. The nearby cottonwood tree is one of the oldest in the Parkway.

Near **Mile 7.4** stands of wild rose compete for sun with wild grape vines. Small rose-colored to light pink flowers appear from May to November. In winter you can sometimes find rose hips, the round seed capsule which has turned bright orange-red. Rose hips are often gathered because they are high in vitamin C, calcium, phosporous and iron. Nisenan also used the juice for red paint.

"Along the rivers there is a strip of bottom–land... where magnificent oaks...cast grateful masses of shade ... And close along the water's edge there was a fine jungle of tropical luxuriance, composed of wild–rose and bramble bushes and a great variety of climbing vines, wreathing and interlacing the branches and trunks of willows and alders, and swinging across from summit to summit in heavy festoons. Here the wild bees reveled in fresh bloom long after the flowers of the drier plain had withered and gone to seed. And in midsummer, when the "blackberries" were ripe, the Indians came from the mountains to feast–men, women, and babies in long, noisy trains, often joined by the farmers of the neighborhood...."
–John Muir

In the summer, butterflies and bees swarm around the wild rose, blackberries, grapes, fennel and morning glories. They are efficient pollinators as they fly from one flower to another. **Honey bees** have an elaborate dance language which describes not only nectar sources but new hive sites.

Bordering the wild rose you can often find Indian tobacco. This plant is a sticky, hairy annual, one to two feet high with narrow oval leaves. White tubular flowers appear from June to August. Nisenan used this plant as smoking tobacco after a meal, before going to bed, or as a social ritual in the sweat house. The only females who used tobacco were the shamans.

As you venture up the trail, can you recognize the dense stands of trees at **Mile 7.5**? In springtime near **Mile 7.6** dark red catkins hang from the branches of a cottonwood tree.

Near the Guy West Bridge, are western redbud trees. Deep pink flowers appear in early spring followed by bronze colored, round leaves which soon turn green. Flat brown seed pods form in July and can still be seen in the winter. The stems and bark were used by the Nisenan in basketry and as decorative coil thread for design and binding. Its darkness contrasted to the lighter colors of willow and reed.

The old town site and fields of **Brighton** are across the river where California State University Sacramento (CSUS) now stands.

Brighton

Brighton was established in 1849 and for three short years had a vivid history. The town was the site of a river landing for schooners, a gambling casino, a race track and the murder of Sacramento's sheriff McKinney during the squatters riots of 1850. The Brighton area eventually became known for hops, wheat, orchards, vineyards, sugarbeets and distilleries.

At **Mile 7.8** pay phones and a convenient cafe are just over the levee on **University Avenue**. Parking is on University Avenue to the north, or for a fee, on the CSUS campus. **Guy West Bridge**, a replica of the Golden Gate Bridge, was named in honor of the first president of Sacramento State University.

Cross the bridge to reach a more than two mile biking and hiking trail along the river to Watt Avenue. This beautiful and historic trail parallels part of the old **Capital City Wheelmen's** and the **Pony Express** route from Sacramento to Folsom. (You can also travel west to H Street on this trail.)

Prior to the mid–1880s many bicyclists rode big–wheeled, hazardous bicycles known as "Ordinaries" and bicycling women wore long skirts and weighted their hems with lead.

SACRAMENTO HISTORY AND SCIENCE ARCHIVES

Bicycles and the 1896 Capital City Wheelway

The ***bicycle*** *was a revolutionary invention. In the days before the automobile, owning a bicycle allowed individuals to get about without the need of maintaining a horse and stable. In 1885 the development of the "safety" model, a fat–tired, single–speed bicycle, caused thousands of bicyclists in the Sacramento area to set up a clamor for decent roads and trails to ride on.*

In April of 1896,500 cyclists rode to Brighton from 31st and J Streets on the new "wheelway." This cinder path was built by the **Capital City Wheelmen**, *Sacramento's first bicycle club formed in 1886. To pay for the path which was to link Sacramento and Folsom, each member of the club was assessed a dollar. Sacramento merchants contributed $900. Later that year when funds began to run out as the trail neared Alder Creek, Folsom merchants kicked in the required sum so the path could be finished.*

Travel onto the Guy West Bridge. Anyone here on a blustery spring day after a storm can still capture that sense of wildness which impressed Jedediah Smith.

A **Pony Express historical marker** *is near the CSUS end of the bridge on the street. The daring young riders of the Pony Express offered "lightening fast" ten day mail delivery*

1860-61

SACRAMENTO HISTORY AND SCIENCE ARCHIVES

service along the 1,966 mile route between St. Joseph, Missouri and San Francisco. Although the Pony Express existed only eighteen months, it transported more than 35,000 letters.

Move southeast along the trail which takes a sharp left turn at the river's bend and travels downhill.

In Alumni Grove locust trees provide shade for picnic tables. Travel under the Sacramento Water Filtration Plant overpass. Near here was Sutter's gristmill, followed by **The Pavilion Hotel** *which burned in the 1850s. This hotel was known for its lively gambling and entertainment imitating the festive atmosphere of Brighton, England. The Brighton horse race course, which also sponsored bear and bull fights, occupied the area to the southwest.*

Continue up the trail toward **Howe Avenue Recreation Area**.

Almost a mile after Howe Avenue an access leads to **Glenbrook Park**. *Between here and Watt Avenue Bridge was the site of the Nisenan village of* **Yusumne**, *which was populated until 1846. Imagine John Fremont's surprise when, after spending weeks wandering in the wilderness, he and Kit Carson saw an Indian building overlooking the river with sun glinting off real glass windows. A western-dressed, Spanish–speaking Nisenan then informed them that Sutter's place was just downriver.*

The **Watt Avenue Recreation Area** *is a popular fishing and raft takeout site. An undeveloped trail leads along the levee from Watt to Gristmill Park. Cross Watt Avenue Bridge to rejoin the Jedediah Smith Bicycle Trail.*

East of Guy West Bridge sycamore trees have been planted. California sycamores grow to 80 feet high and have fuzzy maple-like leaves. In autumn look for the round dangling seed balls. Nisenan used sycamore logs for half-cylinder foot drums and the leaves to wrap food for baking.

Near **Mile 8**, the concrete upright pipe riverside leads to the pump system, transporting sewage under the river to the regional waste water treatment plant.

MILE 8

Up the trail a tenth of a mile, look for the U-shaped set of benches overlooking the river. ***Coyote brush*** *grows on either side of the benches. This large shrub is a valuable plant in the Parkway. When other plants have lost their blooms, coyote brushes' small, whitish blossoms provide food for nectar-loving insects, west coast ladies, blues and buckeye butterflies.*

In autumn and winter, the seeds are an important staple for birds, including western scrub jays. This common, aggressive blue and gray bird feeds on just about anything–acorns, fruit, nuts, seeds, insects, and even bird's eggs and nestlings. Sometimes the acorn or nuts they thump into the ground for a later meal are forgotten and grow into large trees.

At any time of year the quiet observer can also find ***northern flickers*** *here, one of the more than ninety bird species seen in the Sacramento area year–round. Larger than a robin, this brown, black–bibbed bird flashes a white spot on its rump in flight. Its bright orange-red wing and tail feathers make it easy to identify. Watch for the quick "flicker" of red feathers as it dashes between ground and tree where it uses its long sticky tongue to reach insects deep in their nests. Flicker feathers are so unusual Nisenan used them extensively in their ceremonial clothes.*

Looking downriver you can see the ***Sacramento Water Filtration Plant*** *which provides water for domestic use. "Don't dump. Flows directly to creek (or river)" is becoming a familiar sign on the storm drains which line our streets. These signs are part of an effort to keep pollutants from urban runoff out of streams and rivers.*

Near where the water treatment plant is now, in 1848 ***John Sutter*** *had nearly completed a* ***gristmill*** *where wheat from his vast acres would be milled. The mill race was several miles long and began upriver near Gristmill Park. A sawmill had been built in Coloma to supply wood to build the grist-mill. Just before Christmas in 1847, Sutter threw a grand party to celebrate his accomplishments. Wine was freely offered from his cellar. To begin the after–dinner dance, Sutter escorted each lady for a few steps on the dance floor where she was required to sing an improvised verse to the music. But after gold was discovered in the sawmill on January 24, 1848, there was little for Sutter to celebrate and no one to labor over kernels of wheat. Sutter's laborers fled to the gold fields and never finished the gristmill.*

Today not even the old mill stone can be seen. Along with most of Sutter's dreams, it vanished.

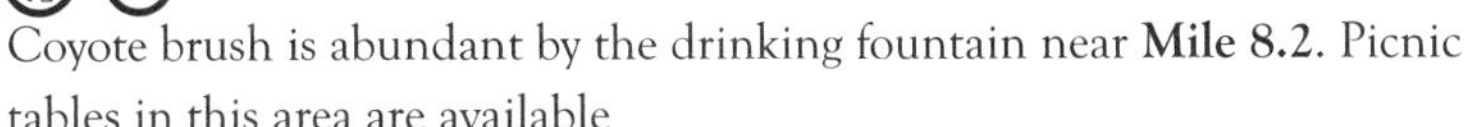

Coyote brush is abundant by the drinking fountain near **Mile 8.2.** Picnic tables in this area are available

Howe Avenue Bridge is at **Mile 8.4.** with an access trail on the northeast leading to University Avenue. The south side of the river is developed for recreation, accessed from the bridge or La Riviera Drive.

You are near where **John Fremont**, with ousted Mexican General Mariano Vallejo in captivity, camped in 1846 during the short–lived **Bear Flag Revolt.** From here Fremont made his way to Sutter's Fort and usurped command because Sutter was thought to have Mexican sympathies. During this almost bloodless war, Fremont and a few hundred American settlers apparently exaggerated Mexican preparations for war so they could wrest California from Mexico.

After the bridge, enter a "forest" of walnut, elderberry and willow trees. Several non-native early blossoming plum and almond trees provide fragrance and color in late winter. During the summer, butterflies, important flower pollinators, enjoy the abundant blossoms in this area. As many as 60 species of butterflies can be found in the American River Parkway from early February to late October. Their colorful wing patterns help attract mates and mislead predators.

At ***Mile 8.5*** *a small trail lined with pungent Mexican tea leads to the equestrian trail and a river overlook. The trees in this area make good bird nesting habitat. Nests are unique to the special requirements of each bird species. The* bushtit nest *is a hanging tube about eight inches long with an entrance hole near the top. Small, plain gray birds with long tails,* bushtits *have a soft twitter and darting behavior. They flock together except during the spring breeding season.*

Along the river bank here is a good place to see horsetail, a biennial rush-like plant. In the time of dinosaurs, horsetail grew almost 100 feet tall. It is one of the last survivors of a group of plants that dominated the earth over 200 million years ago. This multi–jointed plant has stiff, sectioned stems which are rough to the touch. Nisenan and Spanish Californians used this "scouring rush" for cleaning and filing.

Jackrabbits *(black–tailed hares) also abound along Parkway trails. They can jump four feet high to check out intruders or predators such as coyotes, foxes, or raptors and can leap as much as 15 feet in a single jump. Hares and rabbits often rest during the heat of the day by lying crouched in a "form," a slight indentation or matted spot in clumps of grass and weeds. Jackrabbits are really hares with longer ears and legs than rabbits and are born*

fully furred, eyes open, and ready to go. The name came from old-timers who were reminded of the jackass by the hare's long ears, part of their cooling system.

Coyote brush and willow help mark **Mile 9**. Shrubbed areas like these are favorite places for quail, California's state bird. A whit whit, "cuidado" (sounds like "where are you") and whir of wings may surprise you as a covey of California quail darts away. The comma-shaped drooping black plume on the male's head lends a whimsical quality to this plump-bodied, year-round neighbor. Laying up to 12 or more eggs, quail, like rabbits and hares, need to have many babies because they have so many natural enemies.

At **Mile 9.2** picnic benches under cottonwood trees provide a welcome rest stop. Nearby an access trail leads to **Oak Meadow Park** and **Kadema Drive**.

Stands of Poison Hemlock grow north of the trail here. Four to ten feet high, clumps of fern-like hemlock are decorated with clusters of tiny white flowers from May to July. Hemlock was used by the ancient Greeks to execute prisoners. Socrates is one famous example. Every part of this pretty plant is poisonous. In spring and summer, let the stem's purple markings and its musty odor serve as a warning.

The yellow and black anise swallowtail butterfly lays its eggs on sweet fennel, poison hemlock, parsley and other members of the carrot family. These plants then serve as the food source for the larva, a green and black striped caterpillar.

Travel upriver toward Watt Avenue Bridge. At **Mile 9.5** you are near the Nisenan village site of **Kadema**, once located between the river and American River Drive. Kadema was one of two sites on the American River to have a *Kum*, or dance-house, site of important spiritual rituals. A dance house implied wealth in a village because of the necessity of feeding dancers and visitors for indefinite periods. They gambled and played games, enjoying an Indian version of football, which was a "courting" game. The men kicked the ball and the women caught it and ran. The men hugged the woman who carried the ball. When they tickled her, she threw the ball to another woman.

Kademan villager Blind Tom Cleanso refused to leave the village site, even after Haggin's huge horse barns occupied the area. Cleanso proved a rich source of Nisenan history for ethnographer Alfred Kroeber, author of *Ishi*.

Almost at **Mile 10** is **Watt Avenue Bridge**, built in 1959. Restaurants are near the corner of Fair Oaks Boulevard and Watt Avenue. A restroom and drinking fountain are here as well.

NOTES

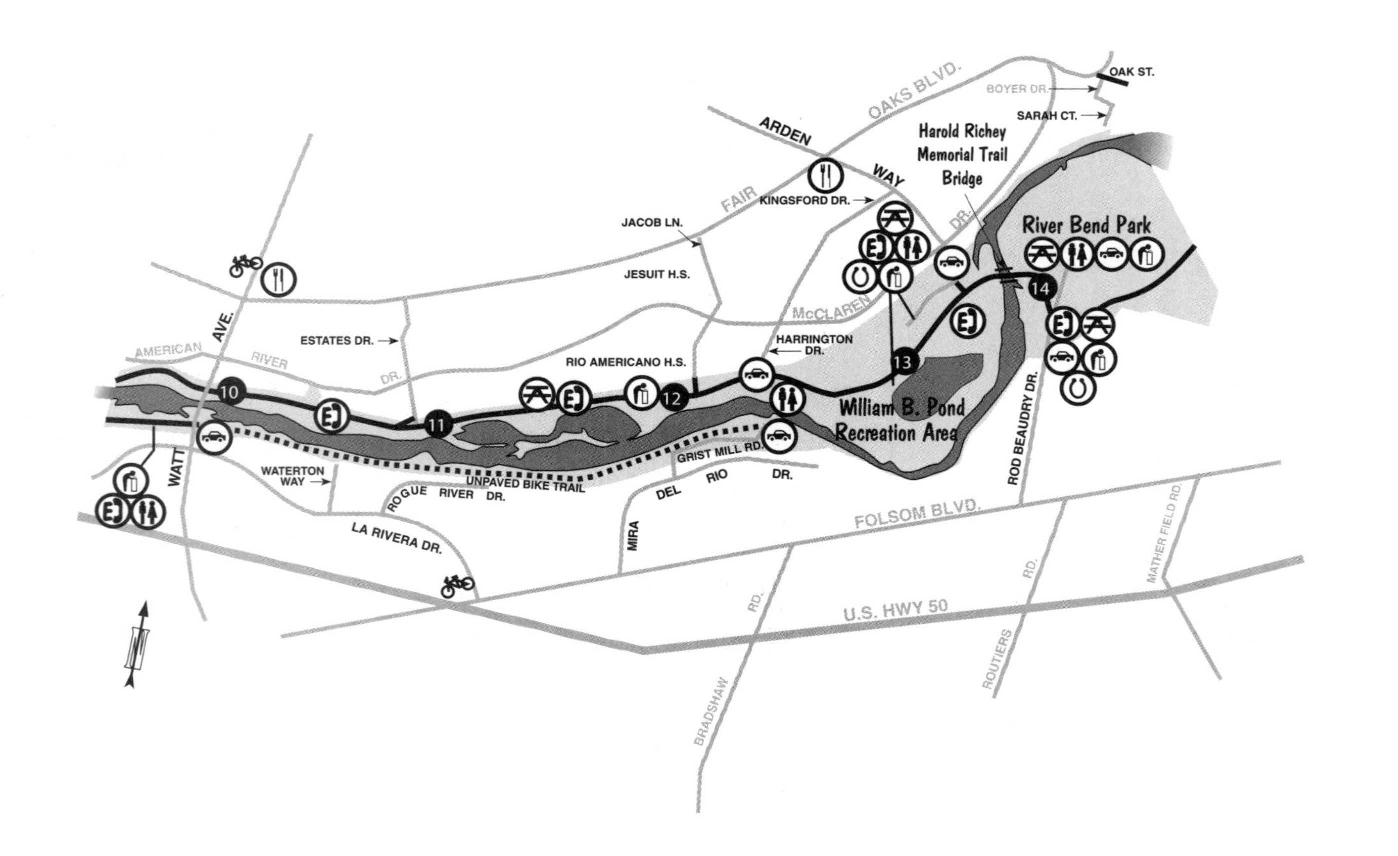

OAK ST.
BOYER DR.
SARAH CT.
OAKS BLVD.
ARDEN
WAY
FAIR
Harold Richey
Memorial Trail
Bridge
KINGSFORD DR.
DR.
River Bend Park
JACOB LN.
JESUIT H.S.
McCLAREN
HARRINGTON
DR.
14
13
ESTATES DR.
AVE.
AMERICAN
RIVER
DR.
RIO AMERICANO H.S.
12
10
11
William B. Pond
Recreation Area
ROD BEAUDRY DR.
GRIST MILL RD.
RIO
DEL
DR.
MIRA
WATERTON
WAY
WATT
ROGUE
RIVER
DR.
UNPAVED BIKE TRAIL
LA RIVERA DR.
FOLSOM BLVD.
MATHER FIELD RD.
RD.
U.S. HWY 50
BRADSHAW
ROUTIERS

WATT AVENUE TO RIVER BEND PARK

Miles 10–13.8

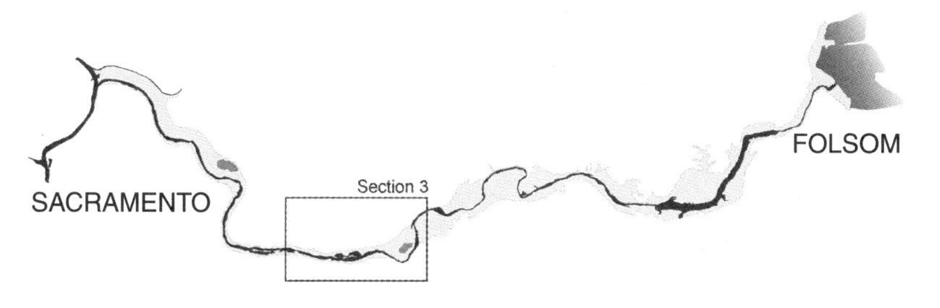

Parkway access is from **American River Drive** on the north or **La Riviera Drive** to the south. Parking is streetside or in Watt Avenue Recreation Area. Restaurants are located near Watt and Fair Oaks Boulevard. A vault restroom and drinking fountain are on the north side of the river.

The next 3.8 miles are a mix of riparian forest; a tree canopy dominated by cottonwood, valley oak and willow; riparian scrub, typified by willow and blackberry; and grasslands, which support non–native grasses and a variety of plants such as star thistle, filaree, vetch and poppy. Star thistle eradication programs are underway in parts of these grasslands. Dredge and gravel mining activities have left open water areas rimmed by rushes, cattails and tules, enjoyed by a wide variety of ducks and fish. As you gain about 20 feet in elevation between Watt Avenue and River Bend Park, the levees will become less prominent. On the south side of the river, an unpaved bicycle trail runs on top of the levee from the Watt Avenue Recreation Area east to Gristmill Park.

RANDY SMITH

A view toward the Sierra from Watt Avenue Bridge.

Mile 10 is just upriver from **Watt Avenue Bridge**. The site of the Teichert building on the north side of the trail was once a huge sand and gravel mining pit. The **Teichert Company** holds California State Business License #8 and is the oldest continuously run business in the state. Since 1887 this large aggregate, land and construction company has managed extensive holdings in the Sacramento Area, including Mississippi Bar in the American River Parkway corridor.

Even though minerals have washed down from the eroding Sierra Nevada for eons, dams have now made lower American River aggregates a diminishing resource.

Up the trail near **Mile 10.3** is a majestic **valley oak tree**. Approximately 150 years old, this oak has grown more than 100 feet high. Many valley oaks have trunks as large as seven feet in diameter and are the highest form of vegetation in the American River Parkway. In winter, having dropped their deeply lobed leaves, the gnarled oak limbs and bared branches make dramatic silhouettes against the sky.

The valley oak produces a sweet **acorn**, but upon drying, it becomes hard and tough and contains less fat than the black oak acorn favored by the Nisenan. Acorns were pounded into a meal which was leached repeatedly to remove tannic acid before being made into cakes, meal or soup.

Near **Mile 10.4** pass over another drainage sump, one of the area's many flood control channels. **SARA Park Area** on the south side of the river begins here. It was named after the Save the American River Association. Near the channel, an import of Mexican origin, poisonous jimsonweed, can often be seen. This large plant has white petunia–like blossoms, stout stems, and grayish fuzzy leaves. The blossoms of summer become big round inedible seeds covered with prickles, hence one common name, thornapple.

Just east of **Mile 10.5** is an access to the levee. To the south, walking trails invite you into an area formerly excavated for sand and gravel.

Near **Mile 11** is the **Estates Drive** access. Street parking is available. A plaque marks the **J. Hagedorn Family Oak Grove.** Jane Hagedorn is one of the founders of the Sacramento Tree Foundation, the California Oak Foundation, and long-time director of Sacramento's American Lung Association (ALA). The many plants and trees in the Parkway's almost 5,000 acres help keep valley air clean by acting as air filters, giving off oxygen and absorbing carbon dioxide.

In the next two miles there are many hiking trails which appeal to those who want to get off the beaten track.

Riparian forest

Walking the trails through this area, you never know what you'll see. Cottontail rabbits sometimes let you come surprisingly close before they scamper into the bushes. Cottontails are gray with light underparts, black-tipped ears and a white puff tail. In spring and early summer, the beautiful blossom of the tall moth mullein may catch your attention. The violet woolly hairs of the stamen provide a striking contrast to the yellow or white flower. Some think the center of the flower looks like the head of a moth. In the fall, most plants like mullein have dried, but you'll find many thickets of square-stemmed blue vervain and mounds of sedge here that are still green. As you round a bend, the delicious scent of a mock orange shrub might greet you, or the scent of another creature not so sweet. The striped skunk is usually an even-tempered animal reluctant to use its formidable weapon, a scent gland located under the tail. As a warning, a skunk may make a few short rushes and stamp its feet. Use this time to back away. The skunk's diet is largely made up of insects, small rodents and fruit.

Great horned owls prey on skunks and other small and medium-sized animals. Though their sense of smell may seem dim, these owls have excellent hearing and sight. The tufts of feathers (horns) at the top of their head make them appear even larger. Their ears are not under these tufts, but are placed on each side of their head, helping them determine distances in the dim of night. These "winged tigers" have feathers adapted for silent flight so they can surprise their prey.

MILE 11

Around **Mile 11** turkey mullein (dove weed), a common, low mounding annual, grows near the trail. Quail, mourning dove and turkeys enjoy its seeds. This hearty, crush-resistant plant is often found in late spring. The fine hairs which cover its grayish-green stems and leaves reduce water loss in the summer and provide insulation during cold weather.

As you travel the Parkway in springtime, you might see a snake sunning in the path. After its winter hiberation, it is absorbing heat from the warm surface in order to hunt longer at night. Snakes "hear" through vibrations picked up from their underbelly in contact with the ground; as a result, it is likely they will know you are there and move out of the path.

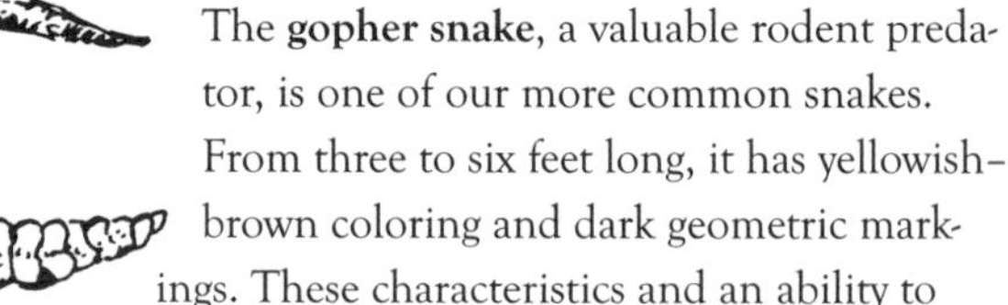

The **gopher snake**, a valuable rodent predator, is one of our more common snakes. From three to six feet long, it has yellowish-brown coloring and dark geometric markings. These characteristics and an ability to flatten its head and shake its tail in imitation of its more dangerous relative, often cause it to be mistaken for our venomous **western rattlesnake**. The gopher snake's slender head and pointed tail, as opposed to the rattler's triangular head and rattle-tipped tail, will help clear up any confusion. Gopher snakes kill prey by constriction, then swallow it whole.

The common kingsnake is another constrictor that preys on rats, mice, lizards, birds—and rattlesnakes. The beautifully banded kingsnake appears quite docile, but will pursue and kill other snakes. It is immune to the rattlesnake's venom. All snakes have a unique way of smelling. A forked tongue flicks out, then plugs into two receptors in the roof of the mouth. If there's more scent of food (or a mate) on the left or right fork, the snake will go in that direction.

Give all snakes a wide berth, or wait until they move off the path.

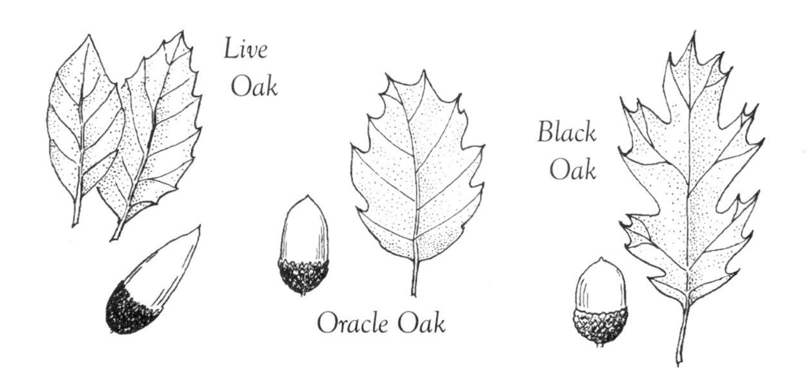

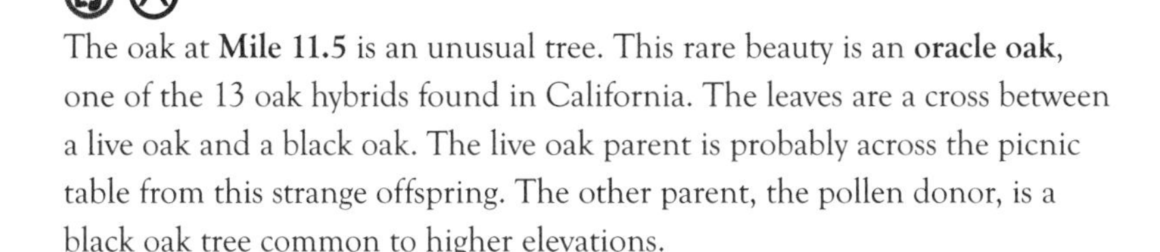

The oak at **Mile 11.5** is an unusual tree. This rare beauty is an **oracle oak**, one of the 13 oak hybrids found in California. The leaves are a cross between a live oak and a black oak. The live oak parent is probably across the picnic table from this strange offspring. The other parent, the pollen donor, is a black oak tree common to higher elevations.

Before the short rise after the equestrian sign is another small trail leading to a site where beavers have been active. In venturing into these hidden areas, show respect for the animals' homes by being quiet and nondisruptive.

Pause along the rise in the trail near Rio Americano High School. From this vantage point you can see nearby lagoon-like river inlets, good places to view ducks and birds during the winter. For more than 25 years, the American River Natural History Association has conducted a Winter Bird Species Count (now expanded into a Winter Wildlife Count) along the American River Parkway. During this one-day count, up to 112 different bird species have been identified.

About one-third of all waterfowl traveling the Pacific Flyway spend the winter in the Sacramento Valley. Migration routes and habits vary with each species. Pintails banded in California have been found as far away as Japan, Siberia, and South America. Mallards wintering here nest in the Columbia River Basin, Canada, and Alaska and usually return to the same nesting and wintering grounds each year. Some mallards can also be seen in the Parkway year round. A few waterfowl, like the cinnamon teal duck, actually migrate to the Sacramento area for the hot summers. Migrating birds are dependent on the River for sustenance.

Take any of the hiking trails in the next quarter mile to the river lagoons to see migrating birds and learn about their connection with the river.

Connections

A river system is almost two rivers, the one you can see above the ground and one below–the groundwater under the river channel. Each interacts with and supplies nutrients to the other. The underground river cleans the river of contaminants, is a refuge for creatures during drought, and serves as a nursery. In a healthy river system, immature stoneflies beneath the surface reign as top predators as they consume smaller prey. Nearer to the surface, fresh-water clams live, filtering the organic soup-of-the-day. The river's underground food chains extend to the surface feeding small organisms, fish and amphibians, and connect with the birds of the sky.

Mile 11.8 is at the access to **Rio Americano High School** and American River Drive.

Moving up the trail, near **Mile 12** you may find ragweed and western raspberry. Western raspberry is a close cousin of the California blackberry though its round, light green stems and leaflets are more slender than those of the blackberry. Like the blackberry, it builds large green prickly mounds, a popular environment for small mammals and birds.

Bewick's wrens and spotted towhees are two birds likely to be seen in the Parkway's berry patches. While most wrens flip their tails up and down, **Bewick's wrens** move their tails from side to side. They have white stripes over their eyes and bodies of dark grayish-brown with whitish underparts. Spotted towhees are as shy as wrens are inquisitive. These towhees have black heads and necks, white bellies and chestnut-colored (rufous) sides. You can sometimes see them as they scratch the ground with both feet at once, looking for insects.

At the **Jacob Lane** access near **Mile 12.2** is a star thistle eradication test area. This stop is a good place to take a closer look into **grasslands**.

If you really want to understand grasslands, you can't just look at them, you need to look into them.

RANDY SMITH

Grasslands

Non-native grasses and thistles that grow rapidly in the brief time between saturation and drought have tended to outcompete native bunch and perennial grasses. Mowing the thistle in May and later in the summer reduces star thistle seed production and allows grasses like wild oats, foxtail fescue, brome and ryegrass, and flowers like poppy, fiddle neck, and the legumes, lupine, clover, and vetch to take hold.

Near **Mile 12.4** is the **Harrington Avenue** access. A fee collection booth marks the entrance into the Harrington Recreation Area. This area and William B. Pond Park are part of the Parkway known as **Arden Bar**. Across the river is the site of Gristmill Park, reached from Mira Del Rio Drive in Rancho Cordova.

Harrington Recreation Area

Travel down the access road toward the river. A combination of history and nature make this area a treat. The park is a popular equestrian staging area, fishing, and river raft takeout point. The sound of the water gliding over the gravel riverbed helps drown out sounds of freeway and city.

Redbud, tree of heaven, and telegraph and jimson weeds brighten the terrain next to the parking area. Near the river off the trail running east, a cottonwood was girdled by beavers and died. Fungi and **western fence lizards (blue-bellied lizards)** *have taken up residence here. Except during their winter hibernation, these brownish–gray lizards are a common site on rotting trees. Blue patches on their bellies become more vivid during the spring mating season. Lizards which lack thick armor, or powerful teeth and claws, have an important means of defense. When caught by a predator, they shed their tail to escape, distracting the enemy by giving it an easy meal. Their habit of pumping up and down upon your approach is their way of saying, "This is my territory."*

Snags are popular nesting sites for tree swallows and European starlings. Tree swallows are the only swallows that can be seen year round in the Sacramento area. The males are steel blue on top and white underneath. Females are more brownish. Look for them skimming over the water, scooping up insects. In March, tree swallows set up housekeeping in numerous tree holes near here, but by April these holes have often been taken over by the invasive, often pesky starling.

Starlings are similar to blackbirds but have shorter tails and heavier bodies. In winter, light flecks mark their black feathers, but by the spring mating season their black plumage flashes brightly iridescent. To attract a mate, the male starling perches outside the nest. With a piece of nesting material in his bill, he repeatedly hops in and out of the chosen nest site. Once the advertisement has worked, the female proceeds to dismantle or discard everything inside the nesting hole and arrange it to her own liking.

Across the river in Gristmill Park was the beginning of the three mile long tail race for Sutter's gristmill.

You can exit the Harrington Recreation Area by continuing east at the parking area and rejoining the bicycle trail upriver at around **Mile 12.6***, or by retracing your way up the hill.*

Up the trail, a "forest" of poison hemlock marks the area with a musky smell. In contrast, for a few weeks in spring, blossoms of black locust trees provide a fragrant bouquet.

Near Mile 12.6 is the **Sand Bar Circle Access.** The land surrounding the decommissioned Northeast Sanitation Plant behind the fencing is now used by the Sacramento Sheriff's Academy. Eventually, this land will be part of the Parkway.

Eucalyptus trees grow on the hill. Their greyish-green leaves are noted for their camphor-like odor. These tall, fast growing trees were introduced from Australia by an enterprising but misdirected pioneer who wanted to supply railroad ties for the budding railroad industry. Unfortunately, the wood twists when dried. Eucalyptus trees become a nuisance when they take over native tree habitat. The high oil content of the leaves prevents other plants from growing under the trees and also makes the trees highly flammable.

On the river side of the trail are remnants of a large gravel quarry. In 1974 funds from a Parkway bond issue allowed the county to acquire these acres from the Arden Sand and Gravel Company before the land was taken over by a 440 home subdivision.

Just west of **Mile 13** an access joins the bike trail leading through **William B. Pond** Park to Arden Way. Restaurants are located at the intersection of Arden Way and Fair Oaks Boulevard.

William B. Pond Park provides facilities located in a grassy landscaped area dotted with sycamore and alder trees. The park was named after the first director of the County Parks and Recreation Department. The American River Parkway Foundation has built and operates a volunteer coordinating center on the site of a former gravel company office building at the Arden Way entrance to the park. Just West of the center is a native plant garden.

At **Mile 13** is a huge stand of Himalaya berry, one of the most common berries in the Parkway. It has larger, pinkish flowers and bigger berries than the native blackberry or western raspberry.

Just upriver is the Arden Pond handicapped-accessible dock and a picnic gazebo. Arden Pond is another quarry left over from aggregate mining days. The bar and islands between the pond and the river were naturally made. Joining the bicycle trail at **Mile 13.3** are excellent hiking and equestrian trails leading into the Arden Pond and Bar area.

Lock your bicycle near the restrooms here and explore this fascinating area.

RANDY SMITH

Aerial view of Arden Bar with Harold Richey Memorial Trail Bridge.

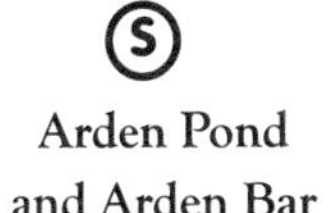

Arden Pond and Arden Bar

Hike on the path which runs toward the river and skirts the main part of **Arden Pond**. *Separated from the river by a gravel dike, the pond supports mosquito fish, bluegills and tule perch, and is periodically stocked with trout and catfish. The abundant pondlife here also includes stoneflies, beetles, crayfish, bullfrogs, tadpoles, damsel fly nymphs, dragonflies, beavers, muskrats and even the elusive otter.*

Islands provide important nesting sites for ducks and other birds. Black phoebes can often be seen in the spring bringing materials to nearby nests. These black and white flycatchers are common year–round residents near ponds, rivers and streams. Listen for the "phee-bee" call.

In the spring, colorful plants dot the trailside which branches toward the pond. Sit quietly amid blue vervain and rushes on a point at the edge of the pond. Rushes grow up to four feet tall in moist and wet places. You can sometimes hear the impatient rattling call of the kingfisher or see patient fishers such as blue heron and egret.

Great blue herons *stand four feet tall and have wings which can span six feet. Watch for their graceful flight, with necks tucked into an S curve and legs trailing behind. Their long yellow bill is a formidable spear. They can also be seen foraging for mice and gophers in drier fields. After feeding, they preen themselves with a soft white powder called powder down which comes from special feathers. You can often spot the dark shadows of great blue heron (and egret) nests in their rookery east of the main pond near the river.*

Another type of fisherman, the more playful variety, will go out of its way to bodysurf a good hill. The adult **river otter** *has a four foot long, streamlined fur-covered body and tail. Crayfish and fish are their favorite foods. Otter scat is recognizable by broken pieces of crayfish shells on logs or river banks. The otter's home is a burrow* *in the riverbank or pond. Adult otters are such skillful swimmers, it may be surprising to learn that young otter pups have to be taught how to swim.*

Hike the trails toward the river into Arden Bar. In the spring, irises rise from their watery home and poke long green stalks with bright yellow flowers toward the sun. Small crustaceans, insects and freshwater clams inhabit the bank. Clam larvae cling to the gills or fins of fish, living as parasites until dropping off to settle on a muddy or sandy bottom. Sometimes a stack of clam shells means a muskrat, otter or raccoon has enjoyed a tasty meal. A muskrat will leave teeth marks on the shells. Tracks or scat will give you other clues. Retrace your steps back to the main trail.

Eppie's Great Race, the "world's oldest triathalon" starts near the tree at **Mile 13.5**. Since 1973 participants have run six miles west to the Guy West Bridge, biked up to the Jim Jones Bridge at Sunrise, then kayaked downriver to River Bend Park across the river.

Travel toward the **Harold Richey Memorial Trail Bridge**. In 1980 this bridge joined the trails on the two sides of the river. Once on the bridge, pull off in one of the overlooks. In the autumn salmon can be seen resting in calm water. They have returned from as far away as Alaska to their spawning grounds here in the American River. Two thirds of the salmon caught off the California coast were spawned in the Sacramento and American River watersheds.

Would you be surprised to see steamships this far up the river? In 1863 when the Sacramento Valley Railroad tracks washed out between here and Sacramento, the steamer *Defiance* met the train from Folsom at Patterson, once located across the river from what is now William Pond Park. In May of 1882 another steamer, the *Daisy*, passed Patterson. Reporting on the slowness of the two day trip, passengers on the ship expected to reach Folsom sometime before next Christmas. Since they were well supplied with roast pig, bread,

RANDY SMITH

Kayakers completing their 12 mile paddle at River Bend Park during Eppie's Great Race.

and butter, they didn't expect to starve. *(The Union.)*

During Eppie's Great Race, boats of another kind stream into **River Bend Park**, just upriver.

Cross the river to River Bend Park.

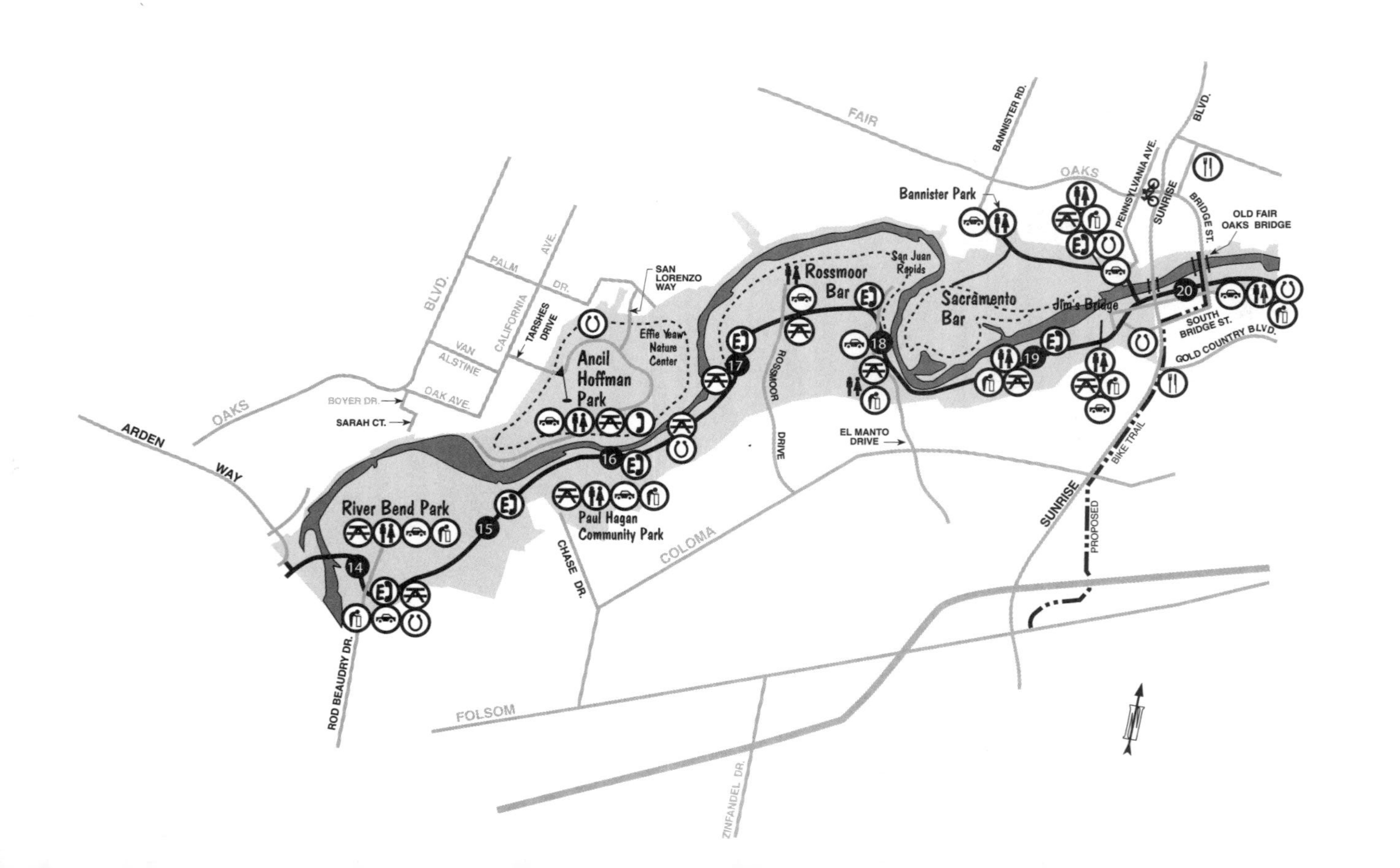

FAIR
OAKS
BLVD.
BANNISTER RD.
Bannister Park
PENNSYLVANIA AVE.
SUNRISE
BRIDGE ST.
OLD FAIR
OAKS BRIDGE
SOUTH
BRIDGE ST.
GOLD COUNTRY BLVD.
Sacramento
Bar
Jim's Bridge
San Juan
Rapids
Rossmoor
Bar
ROSSMOOR
DRIVE
EL MANTO
DRIVE
SAN
LORENZO
WAY
Effie Yeaw
Nature
Center
Ancil
Hoffman
Park
PALM
AVE.
DR.
CALIFORNIA
TARSHES
DRIVE
VAN
ALSTINE
OAK AVE.
BOYER DR.
SARAH CT.
OAKS
BLVD.
ARDEN
WAY
River Bend Park
Paul Hagan
Community Park
CHASE DR.
COLOMA
ROD BEAUDRY DR.
FOLSOM
ZINFANDEL DR.
SUNRISE
BIKE TRAIL
PROPOSED
14
15
16
17
18
19
20

River Bend Park to Sunrise Bridge

Miles 13.80–19.8

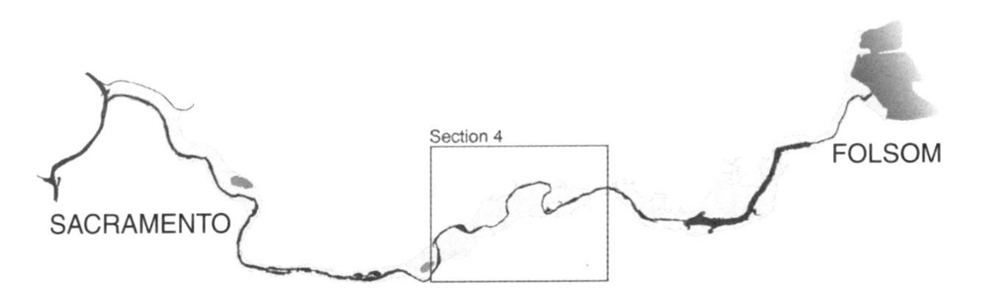

Parkway access at River Bend Park is via **Rod Beaudry Drive** off Folsom Boulevard.

Bicycling and hiking along the six miles of trail from River Bend Park to Sunrise Bridge provides a look at rich riparian, grassland and woodland habitats. The river views and picnic areas in River Bend Park, Hagan Park and in the James Mullaney Grove around Mile 18 make popular destinations. Birders will enjoy the oak woodlands in the Lower Sunrise Area. As the trail winds through furrows of gold tailings at Rossmoor Bar, you'll be reminded of the clank and grind of the mammoth gold dredgers which once chewed through the landscape. The route is an easy one, with just a few undulations and a small vertical rise.

At **Mile 13.8** leave the Harold Richey Memorial Trail Bridge and enter **River Bend Park**. Its 430 acres extend for over a mile, making it the largest park on the south side of the American River. The land for the park was donated by the family of Charles Goethe, philanthropist, writer, and naturalist.

Oaks, cottonwoods and two landmark gray pine trees, unusual at this elevation, shade the large grassy picnic area. The **gray pine** tree was called "gray ghost of the Sierra" by John Muir. The long gray–green needles are three to the bundle and droop from the branches. For all its starkness, its pine nuts are rich in oils and proteins and were prized by the Nisenan. This tree was once called digger pine because of its association with the local native population. Early immigrants had labeled Nisenan "diggers" because they would dig for roots, bulbs, and seeds.

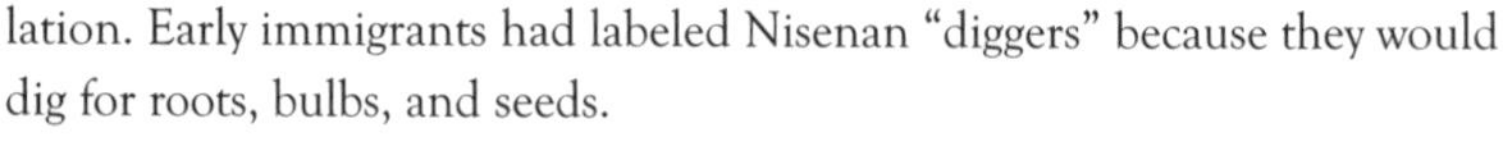

Leaving the river behind for a couple of miles, travel down the slope past the picnic table shaded by a huge valley oak.

Mile 14 is by the intersection of the bike trail and Rod Beaudry Drive. Nearby is one of many good hiking and horse trails that wind through a nature study area. Deer are common here in early morning or evening and mountain lions have made a rare appearance.

Black–tailed deer, a subspecies of mule deer, are year–round inhabitants of the Parkway—and of some neighboring backyards. Their diet includes grass, leaves, and tender twigs and, as gardeners will attest, many things humans have planted. In spring, you can sometimes see young fawns speckled with white spots, good camouflage when they bed down for the day. Mule deer bucks grow new antlers each year and shed them in the winter. To remove the velvet from their new antlers and keep them in good fighting (and rutting) shape, bucks will often rub them on young trees, leaving telltale marks you can identify.

Coyotes are often found in areas like this where they can feed off of weak deer, small mammals, fish, insects, fruits, berries, and reptiles. Coyote scat usually contains hair or fur, differentiating it from dog scat. Their nighttime serenade, a howling and high-pitched yapping, is the "song of the west." They were appreciated by Indians for their secretive and "trickster" nature and hold a revered place in native stories.

Near Mile 14.3 are picnic tables and a drinking fountain near tree of heaven, live oak, and walnut trees. Across the trail, from spring through fall, is milk thistle. This large purple-headed thistle has large white-veined, sharp-spined lower leaves. Thistles provide bees with nectar for a flavorful honey but is not a welcome plant in pastures because it also flavors cow's milk.

Pipevine Swallowtail

As you explore the Parkway, you can often see a familiar vine creeping up elderberry and other small trees. ***Dutchman's pipe*** *grows up to ten feet using trees for support. Its heart shaped leaves, unusual pipe–like blossoms, and relationship to the pipevine swallowtail butterfly make this plant special.*

Dutchman's pipevine is the sole food source of the greenish-black, orange spotted ***pipevine swallowtail butterfly*** *larvae. In spring the butterflies lay their round, rust-red eggs on pipevine leaves. After the eggs hatch, the caterpillar larvae feast on the leaves which become noticeably ragged as summer progresses. Toward autumn, the black and orange caterpillars form a light green or brown chrysalis to overwinter in some protected spot.*

In the spring, dodging the spiny caterpillars can make the shady areas of the bicycle trail an obstacle course. Their secret weapon does not protect them from bicycle tires. Better used to frighten away predators, a Y–shaped fork in the caterpillar's head releases a brightly colored offensive smelling fluid.

A strange invader is found one hundred feet up the trail. The tree with the lumpy green inedible fruit in the summer and fall is an osage orange. Native to southern states, the original home of the Osage Indians, these thorny trees were spread by settlers who planted them as living fences before the advent of barbed wire.

There is one avian Parkway resident often seen near here that has found a use for barbed wire. The loggerhead shrike will sometimes catch a lizard and impale it on barbed wire where the sun turns it into jerky. From a distance, the shrike's black wings and tail make it look like a stocky mockingbird.

Farther along the trail a short way are black locust trees. The levee is off to the southeast of the trail. In the summer, this savannah–like area of grasslands and oak seems so dry it is hard to imagine it flooding. This area burned in the summer of 1997.

Oaks, tree of heaven, and elderberry mark Mile **14.5**.

Sedge

At the bottom of the dip at mile 14.5 is a small dirt trail leading to elderberry trees and sedge. When other plants are dried or burned, sedge remains green. Its deep, water–seeking root system gives it an advantage when water is scarce. In erosion-prone areas, its tenacious roots help keep soil in place, and its "greenness" slows wild fires. Sedge patches were carefully tended by the Nisenan to promote the growth of long roots used in basket making.

The open fields and woodlands up the trail make this a good area for hawks. Searching for prey, they ride thermals for long periods of time, broad wings taking advantage of invisible air currents. Look for the flash of red on the red–tailed hawk and reddish shoulders and banded tail on the smaller red–shouldered hawk. Listen for their high-pitched "tee–urring" screech. The red–shoulder's call is repetitive while red–tails usually make a single call.

Other hawks inhabit the fringes of oak woodlands. Instead of riding thermals, the reclusive Cooper's hawk stays close to cover. This hawk seems to have learned to follow hikers or bicyclists through woodlands. It ambushes smaller birds startled into flight by people on the trail.

Oaks and tree of heaven mark **Mile 14.5**.

Sometimes a stop in an area of seeming wasteland turns up objects of surprising beauty. Choose a tranquil spot where you can test your senses. The quiet might be broken by the cawing of a crow, the tapping of the acorn woodpecker, or the distant rustle of cottonwood leaves. Watch for the purple wings of a tiny lycaenid butterfly dancing between flowering weeds, coyote brush, and thistle.

Near **Mile 14.8** deerweed dots the trailside. Deerweed frequently appears after a fire, becoming an important source of forage for deer and seeds for quail. This bushy plant has small clover-like leaves and seasonal blooms of tiny yellow flowers marked with red. Mugwort surrounds the picnic table.

The fields along the trail at **Mile 15** are part of nearly 250 acres leased from the county for agricultural use. In spring, a variety of flowers like fiddle neck can make these fields a pretty sight. Fiddle neck's orange blossoms are clustered at the top and twisted into a curl, much like the neck of a fiddle. Juicy stems which rot easily when turned under the soil by farmers make it a valuable green compost.

Oaks and elderberries on the river side of the trail are often convenient perches for birds. Flocks of small bright yellow and olive lesser and American goldfinches create a flurry of activity in a tree or weed patch, and feast on star thistle or dandelion seeds. Being beautifully colored like the goldfinch is one of the many ways male birds capture the attention of females. Since the colorful male bird risks getting eaten by sharp-eyed predators but the drab male bird may not get a mate, many male birds wear their most stunning feathers only at breeding time.

Song and dance are another way to grab the attention of the opposite sex. Birds like the male crow, often seen perched on trees in the next few miles of

Parkway, have the technique down pat. When courting, the male bows low to the female, then spreads his wings and tail, and puffs out his feathers, while singing his rattling love song.

After the gunite–lined drainage channel at **Mile 15.25**, you may see ground squirrels perched on the fence watching the passing parade. They are smaller than gray squirrels and have shorter, less bushy tails. Their cheeks also have special pouches often stuffed full of acorns or pine nuts to take back to their burrows. Burrows aerate the soil and help surface water seep underground. They also often shelter toads, snakes, skunks, or burrowing owls.

In contrast to ground squirrels, western gray squirrels have dens in tree cavities or nests of twigs. They jump between trees and ground in search of acorns and can glide up to 20 feet through the air from branch to branch. Thick and bushy tails help them keep their balance. Besides acorns and pine nuts, hungry squirrels will eat tree bark and fungi in the winter, and buds, plant shoots, and birds' eggs in the spring. Like the beaver, the squirrel's front teeth continue to grow throughout its life.

At **Mile 15.5** a look downriver rewards you with an expansive view. Stands of **California (or white) alder** are on the riverbank. This fast growing, water-loving tree has leaves which are green and shiny above and fuzzy yellowish underneath. In January, long male yellow flowers (catkins) hang on the bare twigs. Alders fix nitrogen and add carbon and calcium to the soil around them. Nisenan made a red, brownish, and black dye from alder which they used for coloring skin, bows, arrows or trinkets. Young alder shoots were made into arrow shafts, and the bark was made into as a baby wash for diaper rash.

Across the river is 300-acre **Ancil Hoffman Park**. This popular park contains a championship 18–hole golf course, turfed play and picnic areas, the Effie Yeaw Nature Center, and a 73 acre nature study area. To the first settlers, the Ancil Hoffman Park Area was known as San Juan Meadows, part of the huge San Juan Rancho land grant which extended from Fair Oaks Boulevard and Manzanita Avenue to Auburn-Folsom Road.

Between **Mile 15.7** and **15.9** is **Hagan Community Park's** extensive play and picnic area. A miniature steam-driven passenger train is run by volunteers one Sunday a month at the park's eastern edge. Park access is on **Chase Drive** off Coloma Road.

Adjacent to the Park and bike trail at 2140 Chase Dr., Rancho Cordova, is the **American River Ranch**, the certified organic farm of the nonprofit Soil Born Farm Urban Agricultural and Education Project, and its produce stand. Its mission is to educate children and adults about food, nutrition, sustainable living, and ecological farming.

Along the river, stands of California wild grape cling to oaks and cottonwood trees. These hardy vines can grow more than sixty feet long and sometimes prevent the tree from getting enough sunlight. Fragrant white blossoms become a purple fruit prized by birds, animals and humans. The wide roundish leaves were used to wrap foods for roasting and the stringy bark was used for twine.

Another type of grape was once big business near here. Since crossing the Harold Richey Memorial Trail Bridge, you have been traveling on the old **Rancho Rio de los Americanos**, once owned by William Leidesdorff. When Leidesdorff died in 1848, his 35,000 acre rancho was taken over by Joseph Folsom. Under Folsom's direction, agriculturist Joseph Routier began extensive cultivation of grapes and is credited with the development of the Tokay grape. Wine production lagged when disease hit the vineyards in 1906.

By **Mile 16** you will notice that the levees are nearly gone. The current is swift here, exposing beds of gravel and clay. The strange looking tower across the river is one of several collectors which pump water from below the riverbed for the Carmichael Water District.

Clean drinking water was not always taken for granted along the American River. It wasn't until 1896 that the riverbed level stopped rising due to the slickens and contaminants which kept pouring into the American from gold mining up the river. One early miner complained, "Our drinking water comes to us thoroughly impregnated with the mineral substances washed through the thousand (gold mining) cradles above us." Daniel B. Woods.

River Watch

At **Mile 16.5** *walk the small trail behind the picnic table to the equestrian trail. Head upriver. Just before the junction with the bicycle trail is a small rugged trail to the clay banks at the river's edge. In the fall, salmon use the quiet waters below the bank as a resting spot. Nearby overhanging vegetation and submerged cover provide protection and food, and help keep the water cool. River-loving creatures such as muskrat and belted kingfishers build their nests by tunneling into the river bank. The belted kingfisher's rattling call can be heard as it swoops over the water. This gray, blue and white bird has a large head with a bushy crest and a blue bib (blue and rust for females) around its neck. Unlike bank swallows, who hang their hind end out of the nest to defecate, kingfisher chicks spray their excrement all over their nest, then rap the walls to loosen dirt which covers the waste. When the rising floor begins to crowd them, the young are ready for their first flight.*

Sometimes turkey vultures and gulls can be seen near here. They have come upriver for the fall salmon feed. California gulls are part of the clean–up crew for the American River. When salmon and other pickings are slim, gulls have been known to pound their feet on the ground to draw worms from their homes. The pounding mimics rain to the vibration sensitive worm, triggering a response to surface for air where they are quickly gobbled up.

Crayfish (crawdads) also help with the clean–up job along the river. They live in burrows under rocks or in mud banks like this one. Brownish–green with a smooth exterior shell up to six inches long, crayfish scuttle through the water feasting on small fish, snails, insects or carrion such as dead salmon. They, in turn, sometimes get caught in crayfish traps set up in the river.

Across the river at the eastern edge of Ancil Hoffman Park is the 73–acre **Effie Yeaw Nature Area** and the **Effie Yeaw Nature Center. Effie Yeaw** (pronounced Yaw), a dedicated naturalist and teacher, was instrumental in preserving the area and in the creation of the American River Parkway. The Nature Center provides exhibits and a nature classroom experience to thousands of visitors yearly. Ancil Hoffman Park is reached via Tarshes Road off California Avenue in Carmichael. The Center and Nature Area are funded and managed by the American River Natural History Association, a privately-funded volunteer organization.

As you travel up the trail, you can see that the bluffs along the northern edge of the American River seem to act as a natural barrier, forcing the river to fan, and flood south.

Near **Mile 16.9** is a remnant of the pre–1986 bicycle trail which was destroyed by the spring flood of that year. The new bicycle trail was built on higher ground.

On the river side of **Mile 17** is a large coffeeberry (pigeon berry) shrub**.** These shrubs grow to ten feet high and have velvety grey–green leaves. The small greenish flowers of June and July become round black berries, a natural laxative, particularly loved by wild pigeons.

Interior live oaks are clustered nearby. This common Parkway tree has two kinds of leaves, smooth and toothed. Both are shiny on top with dull undersides. Deer will browse on young leaves, but are somewhat put–off by the points on the sharp, toothed leaves closer to the ground. Take a look at the balls hanging on the area's oaks. **Galls** are growths on stems and leaves usually caused by insects. Each tree has its own type of gall.

Galls

Oak galls *occur when a small wasp of the Cynipidae family lays its egg on the stem of an oak tree. The tree reacts by forming a growth around the egg, providing a nursery for the tiny wasp larva. On the live oak tree, the gall is round with small spikes. On the valley oak, the gall is smooth and round. Jumping oak galls, or flea seeds, are tiny galls found on the underside of valley oak leaves and can make the ground under these oaks a lively place in the fall. As the weather cools, the greenish galls dry and turn brown. Holes in the galls mean the wasps inside have completed their change from egg to larva to pupae to adult, and emerged to begin another cycle. Galls do not harm the tree on which they are formed.*

The trail continues into the **Rossmoor Bar Area**. Over half of the Bar's 855 acres are marked by tailings from gold dredging operations begun after the turn of the Twentieth Century. Before gold dredging changed the topography, flood water regularly cut through the bar at a large sandy channel, making an island of the acreage at its tip. Two state registered archaeological sites near the western border of Rossmoor Bar reveal evidence of Nisenan habitation.

The grassland area to the south after **Mile 17** is a floodplain with the levee far from the river. Look for northern harrier here, white rump patches flashing as they glide low over the ground in search of mice and gophers. Harriers' ground nests are constructed of dry grasses and sedges and make easy targets for coyote, opossum, or raccoon. Western meadowlarks also nest on the ground, hiding their nest under a dome of grass and weed fibers. These beautiful brown and white birds have a black "V" on their bright yellow breast. Meadowlarks feast on many agricultural pests. Listen for their melodious song heralding the beginning of spring.

Another sign of spring in the Parkway is golden field (or yellow) mustard. The large leaves near its base are edible. The oily seeds of mustard are a favorite of song and gamebirds and are the base for our table mustard.

At **Mile 17.3 Rossmoor Bar Road** intersects the bike trail. Where the road ends near the river, you will find parking, facilities, and access to the many horse and hiking trails in this area.

Slightly up the main trail, picnic tables nestle among oak trees. Then for a short distance, a woodland seems to be overtaking the dredge piles. Over time, water and the roots of grasses and plants help break down smaller gravel into soil. As you move up the trail, you can see that dwarf lupine and fiddleneck, grasses, willow, oak and tree of heaven have also begun to reclaim the dredge piles and moisture-collecting depressions. Like the early Chinese immigrants, trees of heaven thrived in inhospitable places and were planted wherever these immigrants camped in the early days of the gold rush—a reminder of home. Their umbrella spread of long compound leaves offers welcome shade to many a hot, dusty area. After its red-tipped leaves have dropped in winter, twisted seed pods hang in dangling groups.

All around **Mile 17.5** are huge gravel piles left from the days of gold dredging. **Dredgers** were huge shovels floating in ponds created as they dug ahead. Acres of land a month were sent through sluice boxes, where riffle devices and mercury separated the gold. A conveyor belt dumped the gravel tailings behind, leaving rows of giant mounds up to 40 feet high. From 1900 to 1962, gold worth billions in today's dollars, was dredged from 17,400 acres of gravels between Sacramento and Folsom.

PHOTO COMPLIMENTS OF FOLSOM HISTORY MUSEUM

Dredgers scooped up gold buried within the earth after the easy pickings were gone.

Mile 17.75 is at the intersection of **El Manto Road** and the bike trail. Parking is at the end of the road near the river. Rossmoor Bar's history, rich habitat, and process of reclamation make it a worthwhile area to explore.

Rossmoor Bar

From either the Rossmoor Bar or El Manto Road parking lots, hikers can make their way to the river to view "swallow cliff." Across the river in a steep bank, rough-wing swallows, ***bank swallows****, and violet-green swallows build their nests in spring.*

More than 47 varieties of birds have been counted along the river here. You might see goldfinches, flycatchers, barn owls, hummingbirds, sandpipers, wrens, terns, killdeer, and mallards.

RANDY SMITH

The San Juan rapids are not far from the El Manto parking lot. These are the only Class II rapids on the Lower American River.

As you move along the trail, look for redstem filaree. This low-growing plant has feathery leaves and springtime pink flowers, followed by beaked seed pods. When ripe, the combination of humidity and sun causes the seed pods to spring loose, twist, and plant themselves into the ground. Filarees provide good grazing for animals and a leafy vegetable for humans. After a hard winter crossing of the Sierra in 1844, Kit Carson and John Fremont's starving party was fed filaree by area natives.

MILE 18

As you approach **Mile 18**, stop at the first set of picnic tables.

James Mullaney Picnic Area

East of the upriver picnic table, look for neat rings of holes in the bark of nearby trees. These holes were made by one of our winter visitors, the red-breasted sapsucker. With its sharp bill it drills into the bark to reach the tree's sap. The sweet syrup attracts insects this resourceful bird adds to its diet. The sapsucker is about the size and shape of our familiar acorn woodpecker, but its entire head and breast are a very bright red. A walk along the trails in this area also reveals blue oak trees, a tree more common to the foothills. This deciduous oak grows to 70 feet high. Its leaves are bluish-green and less deeply lobed than those of the valley oak. In the fall, you can often see migrating salmon and steelhead swimming past the clay banks here. Also watch for the thick oval leaves of ***mistletoe*** *hanging in the trees in this area. Mistletoe draws life from other plants because it lacks sufficient chlorophyll to produce its own food. Seasonal small yellowish flowers turn into white berries attractive to hungry birds. The sticky seeds clinging to the birds' feet help spread this unwelcome guest from tree to tree.*

Other attractive picnic table sites take advantage of the shade provided by the oak trees.

Up the trail at **Mile 18.2** a plaque commemorates **Jedediah Strong Smith** (1799–1831). One of the West's greatest pathfinders, Smith was the first American to venture along the American River and cross the Sierra Nevada and the Great Salt Lake Desert. Despite his wise leadership, the parties he led endured severe hardships and fatal encounters with hostile Indians in both California and the Oregon Territory. Smith survived these, only to be killed by Comanche Indians on the Santa Fe Trail.

From the picnic area here, look across the river into Sacramento Bar. Water-filled ponds left from gold dredges can still be seen.

Near **Mile 18.3** Ambassador Drive connects with El Manto Drive and Coloma Road. You are now entering **Lower Sunrise**, an area of grassy picnic sites, natural marshes, and woodlands continuing up to Sunrise Boulevard.

As you travel this section of the trail in spring, be on the lookout for dwarf lupine in the more wild spots or on the river islands. Dwarf lupine has the legume family's characteristic bonnet-shaped flower and is bluish-purple trimmed in white. Part of their scientific name, *lupinus,* means wolf. This name was chosen because of a mistaken idea that since lupines are often found growing in poor soils, they rob the soil of nutrients, as wolves are thought to do with their prey.

At a sharp bend toward the river, the trail leads you into a rare woodland habitat. The next mile offers some of the best birding along the American River Parkway.

Oak Woodland

In the spring and fall, many song birds such as the yellow-rumped warbler and the western tanager shelter here during their migrations. In spring and summer, this area is alive with the sound of bird calls. Most birds sing primarily during the mating and nesting season to impress a mate and establish their territories. Other calls may indicate alarm, food, or signal to their brood. Listening, then observing the bird's behavior, can tell you what's happening.

As fall nudges summer out of the way, the leaves behind which so many birds and animals have found cover, color and die. Losing their leaves decreases the weight and wind resistance of limbs and allows the now dormant trees to avoid periods of poor growing conditions. Live oaks lose just some of their leaves in the winter, causing natives to call it the tree that sleeps with one eye open.

The trees here have provided acorns that were sustenance to the Nisenan, filled woodpeckers' granaries and scrub jays' caches–and fattened bears. Though the grizzly bears which frequented the valley are extinct in California, John Fremont

ROBIN DONNELLY

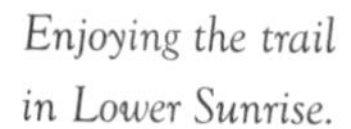

Enjoying the trail in Lower Sunrise.

reported how he sighted grizzly cubs in the upper boughs of valley oaks breaking off the smaller branches which carried the acorns and throwing them to the ground.

Early settlers found that the presence of valley oaks indicated another type of wealth–deep rich soil. As agriculture and grazing developed in the mid–1800s, oak forests were destroyed by the thousands of acres. Since a third of all mammals in California depend on oaks and the plants that grow with them for food or nesting sites, Sacramento County now has a tree ordinance forbidding the unauthorized cutting of any native oak with a trunk larger than six inches.

In the middle of this oak woodland near **Mile 18.5** is a grassy area for picnicking. The restroom has been closed due to repeated vandalism. Upriver 100 feet is a snag that is an **acorn woodpecker stash**. Being able to store food means this bird is able to avoid the hazards of migration. When the acorns shrink and dry, they are often moved to better-fitting holes by custodial woodpeckers whose job it is to oversee the communal warehouse for the flock. As bugs and weevils infest the acorn, the meal becomes even more nutritious. The black and white face markings and red cap of the acorn woodpecker make it one of the Parkway's most popular sightings. White patches on wings and rump flash as it swoops from tree to tree. Acorn woodpecker feathers brightened Nisenan headgear, belts, earrings, and baskets.

After **Mile 19** is another shady picnic spot. From here an easy walk along the river brings you to the remains of two giant cottonwood trees.

Big Bertha

Walk to the river and turn upriver on the equestrian trail. Along the trail, a cottonwood snag, Big Bertha, was considered the oldest and largest of its species in Sacramento. Miniature plants, tiny algae, fungi, lichens, mosses, and liverworts now live on its decaying wood, quietly unlocking nutrients for other growing plants to use. This trail continues toward a seasonal pond where beavers are often active .

Near the **Park Road** access up the trail, you will find large stands of sweet fennel and milk thistle intermingled in a live oak and elderberry restoration project.

The bicycle trail curves toward the river at Sunrise Boulevard.

JIM JONES

Jim's Bridge

Near **Mile 19.7** is **Lower Sunrise Park**, a favorite spot for salmon viewing, sunbathing, swimming, and raft launching. At the intersection, the trail branches off to **Jim's Bridge**, a popular pedestrian and bicycle crossing. Jim Jones has been a champion of the river for many years. When the gravel miners left and Lower Sunrise became part of the Parkway, he persuaded the Board of Supervisors to retain this old bridge. The bridge was originally built to handle the trucks of the Lone Star Gravel Company, which mined gravel along the river here until 1975. At times of heavy flooding the bridge is submerged, and the onramps tend to get washed out.

Ⓢ
Sacramento Bar

Cross Jim's Bridge to **Sacramento Bar** *and prime, shaded picnicking grounds. The main accesses on the northside of the river are* **Pennsylvania Avenue** *and* **Bannister Park**. *A sidetrip into the Bar's nature area is a worthwhile venture.*

Follow the bike path west toward Bannister Park to find trails leading through a heavily dredged, but serene area to the San Juan Rapids. Sacramento Bar, the last gold dredging field on the American River, was operational until 1962. A fishing pond has been developed from one of the holes left by the dredging operation. Minnesota Creek runs through Sacramento Bar, helping make early morning or evening birding excursions rewarding.

Another good reason to explore Sacramento Bar is because it is one of the few places on the Parkway with good stands of **milkweed.** *Milkweed is easiest to recognize in summer when its deep pink or maroon petals are folded away from the flower's pale pink center. Both the leaves and the pale, velvety grayish-green stems are covered with woolly hairs. The seeds, aided by a parachute of fluffy white fibers, can float long distances on the wind.*

Members of the milkweed family are the sole host plant for the monarch butterfly larvae. **Monarch butterflies** *have reddish-brown wings bordered by black with two rows of small white spots. The yellow, black, and white caterpillars feast on the plant's bitter poison which makes both the larvae and adult insect distasteful to birds. In mid-October, after completion of their summer breeding cycle here, monarchs head for the beach–communal wintering sites on the coast around Pacific Grove, Santa Cruz, Morro Bay, and Pismo Beach.*

Nimbus Overlook
Nimbus Flat
CSUS A
Cente
Sailor Bar
Nimbus Hatchery
Fair Oaks Bluff
Jim's Bridge
OLD FAIR OAKS BRIDGE
BRIDGE ST.
SOUTH BRIDGE STREET
NATOMA AVE.
OLIVE AVE.
WINDING
WAY
ILLINOIS
AVE.
SUNSET
AVE.
HAZEL
AVE.
SUNRISE
BLVD.
PENNSYLVANIA AVE.
OAKS
GOLD COUNTRY
BLVD.
SUNRISE
BIKE TRAIL
SUNRISE
U.S. HWY 50
FOLSOM SOUTH CANAL RECREATION TRAIL (14 miles)
To Cosumnes River
20
21
22
23

Sunrise Bridge to Hazel Avenue

Miles 19.8–23

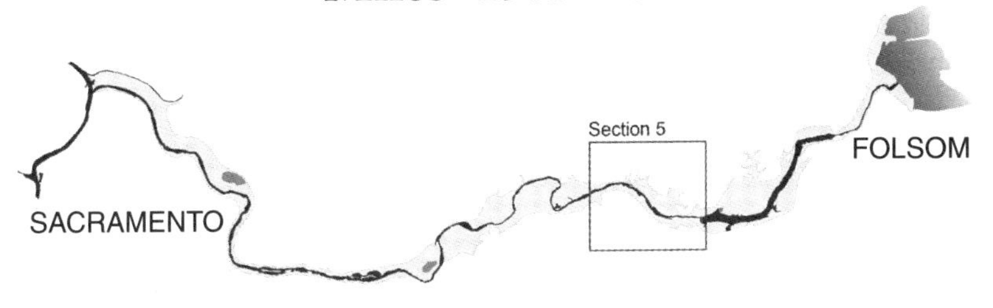

Access between the Parkway and Sunrise Boulevard is at **South Bridge Street** (off the east side of Sunrise) at American River Raft Rentals. Cafes and restaurants are a quarter-mile south off Gold River and Sunrise Boulevards.

The three miles in this section are in the **Upper Sunrise Area**, extending from Sunrise Bridge to the state owned Nimbus Fish Hatchery at Hazel Avenue. Woodlands have begun to reclaim the terrain where extensive gravel mining and gold dredging took place. Nisenan and Chinese ruins have also been found. The higher riverbanks are the beginning of foothill country so you'll start to see some species not found lower in the Parkway. Walking trails take best advantage of the panoramic views and the natural and historic areas. Several good sidetrip options are at Hazel Avenue.

At **Mile 19.8** continue east on the bicycle trail under **Sunrise Bridge**. In the spring, cliff swallows have found the underside of the bridge an ideal place to build their mud nests and raise a family. You can identify them by their dark chestnut throat, dark head, pale forehead, square tail, and yellow-orange rump. Sacramento's cliff swallows, like their famous San Juan Capistrano relatives, return from southern climates to the Sacramento region within a few days of March 10 each year.

Under the bridge and along the trail look for **tree tobacco**. This shrub-like tree is quick to take over where soil has been disturbed. It has smooth oval leaves and, in spring and summer, showy clusters of trumpet-like greenish-yellow flowers. Hummingbirds find the nectar of the flowers a welcome addition to their diet. Like other tobacco plants in the genus *nicotiniana,* the leaves of tree tobacco are poisonous to eat, whether cooked or raw. *Nicotianas* were named for the French Ambassador to Portugal, Jean Nicot, who introduced tobacco to France about 1560.

On the eastern side of Sunrise Bridge, the trail passes over **Buffalo Creek.** You cannot see much of this channeled creek until it floods after a heavy rain. It overflowed in the spring of 1995, washing out this section of the bicycle trail. Lone Star Gravel Industries mined this area until the 1970s. When you look at the photograph taken in 1924, you can see the amazing amount of reclamation that has occurred.

BOB BRUGGER

The view northwest of gravel mining near Old Fair Oaks Bridge, 1924. The Fair Oaks Bridge railroad depot was near what is now an auto dismantling shop off South Bridge Street.

At **Mile 20** is **California mugwort,** a common native plant whose springtime lush, deeply incised leaves give way to smaller leaves better able to withstand intense sun and heat. Mugwort has a strong, but pleasant odor. Nisenan found that mugwort's pungency made a good insect repellent. They found it useful for keeping bugs out of acorn granaries. Mugwort rubbed on the sweaty skins of hunters would also help disguise their human scent and serve as a poultice for poison oak rash.

As you travel up the trail in late spring, look for grass pink near the access trails to **Old Fair Oaks Bridge**. Grass pink has linear leaves and a tight cluster of small pink buds on top. After the flowers have withered, dozens of tiny black seeds can be shaken out of their papery wrapping. The new Sunrise Bicycle Trail begins here and continues south to Folsom Boulevard.

Fair Oaks Bridge, built in 1908, connected Fair Oaks to Coloma Road and a railroad depot on the south side of the river. After Sunrise Bridge was opened in 1964, the old bridge became the property of the Sacramento County Parks and Recreation Department. Redecked and opened to bicyclists, pedestrians, and equestrians in 1973, the bridge has been both a popular destination and a handy river crossing. The village of Fair Oaks is across the river up Bridge Street.

The old Fair Oaks Bridge was a popular byway. Here some Capital City Wheelman enjoy the view.

SACRAMENTO HISTORY AND SCIENCE ARCHIVES

Travel across the ***Old Fair Oaks Bridge****, taking time to read the historical plaque on the north side of the bridge, and continue to the old town of Fair Oaks.*

Fair Oaks

Several restaurants, shops, an art school and gallery, a public square, and other attractions maintain the ambience of the old colony..

Fair Oaks, the second major colony begun on the San Juan Grant, was established in 1895 when promoters brought 106 prospective land owners on board an excursion train from Chicago. The settlers were attracted by the ideal climate and moderate cost ($100–120 an acre). Water was hauled up from the American River in barrels until July 1896 when a leaky pipe was laid along the town's main street. From this early beginning in 1895 to the big freeze of 1932, the heavily wooded colony of Fair Oaks was turned into lemon, orange, almond and olive orchards as oaks were cut down and replaced with fruit trees.

Pigeons roost among the grapevine covered wooden struts of Fair Oaks Bridge. In urban areas the pigeon population sometimes soars out of control, but here natural predators keep the pigeon population in balance.

Look for bat guano under the close-together bridge rafters on either side of the bicycle trail. The Mexican free–tailed bat, one of the species residing here during the warmer months of the year, has narrow wings and is a fast, erratic flyer. Bats make up about one–quarter of all the mammal species in the world, but their numbers have declined due to harassment and loss of habitat.

From the river bank you can see **Fair Oaks Bluff** on the north side of the river. Hanging over the cliff are tenacious craggy oaks. This is the last piece of scenic bluff accessible to the public along the American River Parkway. The panorama stretches from the snow-capped Sierra to Mt. Diablo. In 1999-2006, Citizens to Save the Bluffs, a local grass-roots organization, raised 1.3 million dollars to buy the Bluff and keep it for public use. A hiking trail crosses the property and a donor plaza with interpretive signs is planned for the property. It is a premier spot from which to watch the sunrise and sunset.

Some of our most beautiful year-round avian residents, **great egrets,** seem to find the winter fishing especially good in the next stretch of river. Their long sharp yellow bills and long black legs make them well adapted to fishing. Standing patiently or wading slowly through the water, they spear fish with a sudden lunge. Snowy egrets are smaller with a dark bill and yellow feet. It is said this egret sometimes wiggles its yellow toes to mimic worms so that fish will come close to investigate.

Great egret reflecting an early morning meal.

DAVID ROSEN/DUCKS UNLIMITED

Cottonwood, live oak, and tree of heaven grace the trail for the next quarter mile. Near **Mile 20.4** the park road parallels the trail.

Along the trail are plants adapted to hot, dry places. Telegraph weed, Mexican tea, jimsonweed, and the pungent virgate tarweed have hairy stems and leaves which help them conserve water.

Common mullein's coat of interlacing hairs is collected by hummingbirds for their nests. This mullein spends its first year as a lowly rosette of large grayish leaves. In its second year, it sends up a tall stalk with yellow flowers. In the fall, the spike appears very dry with a curly top, yet its abundant seeds furnish a timely banquet for goldfinches.

Near **Mile 20.5** is a path to the park road. Slightly upriver, a quarter-mile hiking trail lets you meander under majestic valley oaks before eventually rejoining the bike trail.

Ⓢ Oak woodland

Take the dirt trail to the south of the bicycle trail. As you enter the woodland, open your senses to its sights, smell, and sounds. This is a good area to look for Nuttall's woodpeckers and tiny oak titmice. ***Nuttall's woodpecker*** *has a striped black and white back. The male has a red patch on its head. Listen for a rattling "prrrrt" or the familiar tapping sound that will tell you it is near. The oak titmouse is a tiny gray bird with a little crest on its head. This agile bird twists around limbs searching for insects, berries and seeds. Clumps of miner's lettuce are a winter and early spring treat. Round leaves encircle a stem that bears seasonal small white or pink flowers. Just past the old gravel plant concrete structure and down the hill, join with the main trail near* ***Mile 20.8****.*

Near **Mile 20.6** picnic tables nestle among live oaks. Up the trail a clearing at the river's edge is surrounded by blue vervain. This common, square-stemmed plant grows up to seven feet tall along the river and in other moist places. Spikes of tiny, bright lavender-blue flowers bloom in summer.

In the autumn, this spot is one of the best places to see salmon and steelhead spawning in the river riffles.

Spawning Time

Many of the salmon and steelhead swimming up the American between September and January spawn in the gravel riffles between Ancil Hoffman Park and Nimbus Dam. ***Chinook*** *(or king) salmon range from three to 70 pounds with an average weight of 15 pounds. Their bodies are dusky above and silvery below with black spots along their sides and fins. By the time these migrants have come this far upriver, they are host to a relatively harmless whitish fungus.* **Steelhead** *are rainbow trout which have gone to sea. They are usually smaller than salmon, more heavily spotted, and have a reddish stripe. Though they spawn much like salmon, they do not die afterward but make their way back to the sea. Spawning occurs when a female digs a hole with her tail in clean pea-sized gravel and lays her eggs. A male fertilizes them, and then covers the fragile eggs with gravel. With an ample supply of fresh, cool water, the eggs hatch in about two months.*

Turkey vultures *and gulls are often watching for a salmon meal. Turkey vultures can be identified by their black feathers and bald red heads, well–suited for their messy job. Vultures use their sharp eyes and sense of smell to find the dead animals that make up their meals. They sometimes follow other vultures spiraling down from the sky in formations called kettles.*

DAVID ROSEN/DUCKS UNLIMITED

Birds like cormorants and these turkey vultures spread their wings to dry.

Near the trail rise after **Mile 20.7**, the 15-foot high concrete structure south of the bike trail is part of a gravel mining pumping station where water was taken from the river to wash the aggregate.

In late summer and fall, the white berries of common snowberry look like dots of light near the path leading into the woods. This graceful shrub grows two to six feet high. In spring, its slender branches sprout roundish leaves and then pink bell-shaped flowers.

Mile 20.8 is a favorite stop with picnic tables shaded by valley oaks. Elderberry trees have Dutchman's pipevine intertwined in their branches. Across the trail is a fungus covered fallen tree and a redbud. In early winter a lush crop of miner's lettuce lines the trail.

The equestrian trail crosses the main trail here and weaves off into a network of beautiful and historic paths.

Chinese Mining and Sunrise Day Camp Sites

Take this trail into the woodland to the rocky foundations left by the ***Chinese*** *who built ground sluices and a mining camp in this area. By the mid-1850s political turmoil and economic hardship in China, coupled with news of gold and good wages in California, caused thousands of Chinese to flee to the gold fields. Once here, they often kept their language, appearance and customs intact. One custom which served them well was their habit of drinking tea. The boiled water killed the dysentery germ responsible for sickness and death among many other miners.*

The rocky ledges of these nearly hidden ruins now make good homes for bush monkey flower and the occasional bracken fern. Young fronds, known as fiddleheads, were boiled or tossed into stews by both miners and natives. The large triangular fronds were also used by Nisenan for thatching roofs and the hairy rootstocks were woven into baskets and clothing.

Near the center of this area, picnic tables make good outposts. A few foothill bird species such as the phainopepla can sometimes be spotted. This shiny black bird has a jaunty crest and red eyes. Another visitor is the white–breasted nuthatch. This small bird has a black cap, a gray back, and white underparts and works its way head–first down a tree as it hunts for insects. Up the trail, you find the old Sunrise Day Camp ampitheater filled with lupine in the summer. Continue to the main bicycle trail or meander on the paths that weave through this area.

As you move up the rise, **Mile 21** is just east of an access road from Gold River. Gold dredge tailings, reminders of the past, contrast with the rooftops of the Gold River residential development.

Upper Sunrise is one of the few areas on the Parkway where the showy wildflower Indian paintbrush can be found. Thriving in the cobble piles left from dredgers, the fuzzy stems and leaves protect this plant from heat and cold on the dry slopes and in rocky crevices. The blossoms themselves are inconspicuous but they are surrounded by colorful bracts (leaf parts) that form reddish–orange, dense spikes.

Near **Mile 21.2** is another access to the park road and the Sunrise Day Camp area.

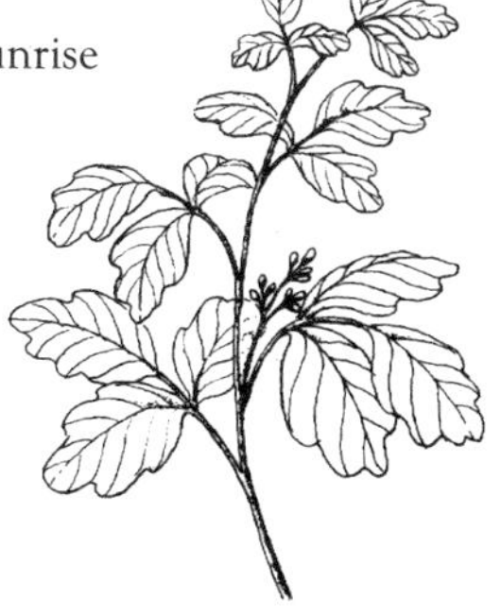

At **Mile 21.4** a stand of poison oak is on the northeast corner of the path leading to some picnic tables with a river view. **Poison oak** grows as a two to eight foot shrub, or a 15 to 40 foot vine. Three glossy green leaflets on each stem warn of the unpleasant skin rash you can develop after contact. Tiny greenish–white flowers become berries as the summer wanes and in fall the leaves turn red. Watch out for this common, everchanging valley native.

Don't touch! The rule is—leaves in three, let them be.

Winter is a time to use your binoculars. Keep them handy as you walk on the trails above the river for a close up of a favorite winter migrant, the common goldeneye. The male has a round white spot below the eye. The female's head is lighter, with a white collar instead of a facial spot. As they fly low over the water, their wing beats make a whistling sound—earning them another name "whistler." They float the river currents searching the river bottom for their favorite foods, shellfish, and snails.

Across the river is **Sailor Bar**, named after a sailor who jumped ship and established a claim. The Bar's 375 acres are rich in cultural and natural history and offer horse and nature trails, picnic areas, fishing sites, and access for rafters and boaters. Grinding holes made by Nisenan in the riverside hard pan indicate an old camp with a plentiful supply of acorns nearby. The riffles upriver would have made a good location to stretch a willow salmon weir across the river or to use a salmon spear.

Sailor Bar

If you are on the north side of the river, you can travel to **Sailor Bar** by taking either the western access at Olive Avenue or the main access at Illinois Avenue off Winding Way. Off the main access is evidence of hydraulic mining, the only area on the lower American River where this type of mining occurred. A giant water gun, called a monitor, allowed whole hillsides to be blasted away, sending tons of debris into the river. Hydraulic mining was banned in 1884, the world's first major environmental legal decision.

The fishing pond located near the Illinois entrance may be part of a ditch system which fed the monitors. Today, **pond turtles** bask on logs, and muskrats swim between the tules. Mallards and migrant ducks feast among the yellow pond weed and cattail. North of the pond is an 80–acre woodland area that is excellent for birding and native plant identification.

This area is also one of the few places on the Parkway where small stands of once-common bunch grasses still exist. Bunch grasses, such as purple needlegrass, are perennials that expand from the base by producing new stems as well as spreading to new sites with windblown seeds. When livestock overgrazing removed all the above–ground leaf parts needed for reproduction, these native grasses began to die out, and introduced grasses like wild oats, fescues, and ryegrass took over.

Travel toward the river to one of the many parking areas in the Bar. In the fall, river riffles are a good place to view spawning salmon. You can find the Nisenan grinding holes near the river's edge east of the alder tree, a few minutes walk west of the boat launch.

Near **Mile 21.5**, bush monkey flower provides one of the most commonly seen splashes of color in the upper portions of the Parkway. Two to four feet high with dark green sticky stems and leaves, the long-necked yellow-orange flowers bloom from April through October.

Up the trail, buckeye trees may capture your interest. Early in the spring, the white flower spikes of the buckeye trees look like feathery plumes against winter's dull wardrobe. Yet when other bushes and trees are still green in late summer and early fall, the buckeye's large palmate leaves appear brown and dead. The leaves do not hold up well to summer's heat, so they have adapted to sprouting in winter and making an early exit, leaving the pear-shaped buckeye nut to hang on bare branches.

At **Mile 21.8** is an access to **Gold River**.

Sluices

Sluices, thought to have been built by Chinese miners, divide the landscape next to the river. A canal fed water into these trenches to wash out the gold. Quicksilver (mercury) was added to sluice riffles to collect the gold.

Now Chinese tree of heaven, common mullein, California fuchsia, coffeeberry, bush monkey flower, deerweed, and coyote mint cling to the edges of these sluices. Coyote mint grows in dry areas. Its square stems reach about one foot in height. Though its showy purple blossoms don't appear until June or July, a minty fragrance can be enjoyed year-round. In moist places are shooting stars. Their lavender to maroon flower petals turn back, revealing a band of maroon and yellow.

At **Mile 22.5** is the Nimbus American River Trout Hatchery followed by the **Nimbus Fish Hatchery**. Proceeds from sales of fishing licenses help these facilities to raise fish for release into rivers and lakes.

The Nimbus Fish Hatchery

***The Nimbus Fish Hatchery**, built in 1955 by the U.S. Bureau of Reclamation, is an artificial nursery to partially substitute for salmon and steelhead spawning grounds lost after the completion of Folsom and Nimbus Dams. The hatchery offers tours and an interpretive center.*

The American River between Ancil Hoffman and Nimbus Dam is closed to fishing each autumn to protect the fish that make their way upriver and into the hatchery. Here salmon are anesthetized, killed, and the eggs and sperm removed. Steelhead are milked and released because, unlike salmon, they can return to spawn several times during their lives. The eggs are stored in incubators until they develop into fry. Around June, in a good year, millions of small salmon and steelhead smolt are then released into the Sacramento River at Rio Vista. In a few years many will return from their ocean home and fight their way up the American River to the place of their birth.

From the hatchery the bicycle trail merges briefly with **Nimbus Way**. At **Gold Country Boulevard**, the trail bears left towards Hazel Avenue. Across the boulevard is the **Folsom South Canal Recreation Trail**, managed by the Bureau of Reclamation. The canal and its accompanying unmarked trail extend 14 miles from Nimbus Dam to Sloughhouse Road.

Folsom South Canal

*The **Folsom South Canal** was initially planned to be 69 miles long with an initial water diversion capacity of 3,500 cubic feet per second, or about the amount of water that flows down the American on an average summer's day. The Save the American River Association and the Natural Resources Defense Council blocked completion of the canal. Recently, members of the Sacramento Area Water Forum reached an agreement which will allow the East Bay Municipal Utilities District (EBMUD) to pull American River water from near the confluence of the American and Sacramento Rivers instead of from the present inlet to the* *canal. Presently, the canal extends to Rancho Seco where it continues to supply water to the decommissioned (but still hot) nuclear power plant.*

Across **Hazel Avenue** on the south side of Lake Natoma are the **CSUS Lake Natomas Aquatic Center** and **Nimbus Flat Day Use Area,** both part of Folsom Lake State Recreation Area.

Ⓢ

CSUS Aquatic Center and Nimbus Flat Day Use Area

Cross Hazel Avenue into the ***CSUS Aquatic Center*** *operated by California State University, Sacramento, through an agreement with State Parks. The center provides instruction and/or rentals for sailing, water skiing, canoeing, kayaking and rowing. (Call 985–7239)*

South on Hazel Avenue over the Folsom South Canal Bridge is the entrance to ***Nimbus Flat****. In a clearing midway into the park is an historical marker for the* ***Old Coloma Road****, established in 1847 to serve as a supply route from Sutter's Fort to the sawmill in Coloma. After the discovery of gold, thousands of people traveled the road going to and from the "diggins." They didn't need to know the road, but instead, followed a trail of bottles strewn along the whole way.*

East Lake Natoma Trail

Travel east to the new picnicking grounds. A grassy play area and water sports make this an attractive spot. At the eastern end of the developed area is a handicapped–accessible fishing pier. A hiking and bicycling trail is planned along the south shore of Lake Natoma which may eventually connect to the the town of Folsom and the Humbug–Willow Creek Trail.

the town of Folsom and the Humbug–Willow Creek Trail.

At **Mile 22.8** is **Hazel Avenue Bridge**, built by Sacramento County in 1966. Until trail improvements are completed, the separated equestrian trail on the west side of the Hazel Avenue bridge is the route often used by bikers and hikers to cross the American River.

In fall and early winter you can see a weir, a wire mesh fence that drops across the river, so salmon will be forced into the hatchery. The only fish found above the weir are those that came before the screen was lowered or those able to squeeze through the openings.

After crossing the bridge, travel cautiously down the access paths to the bicycle trail.

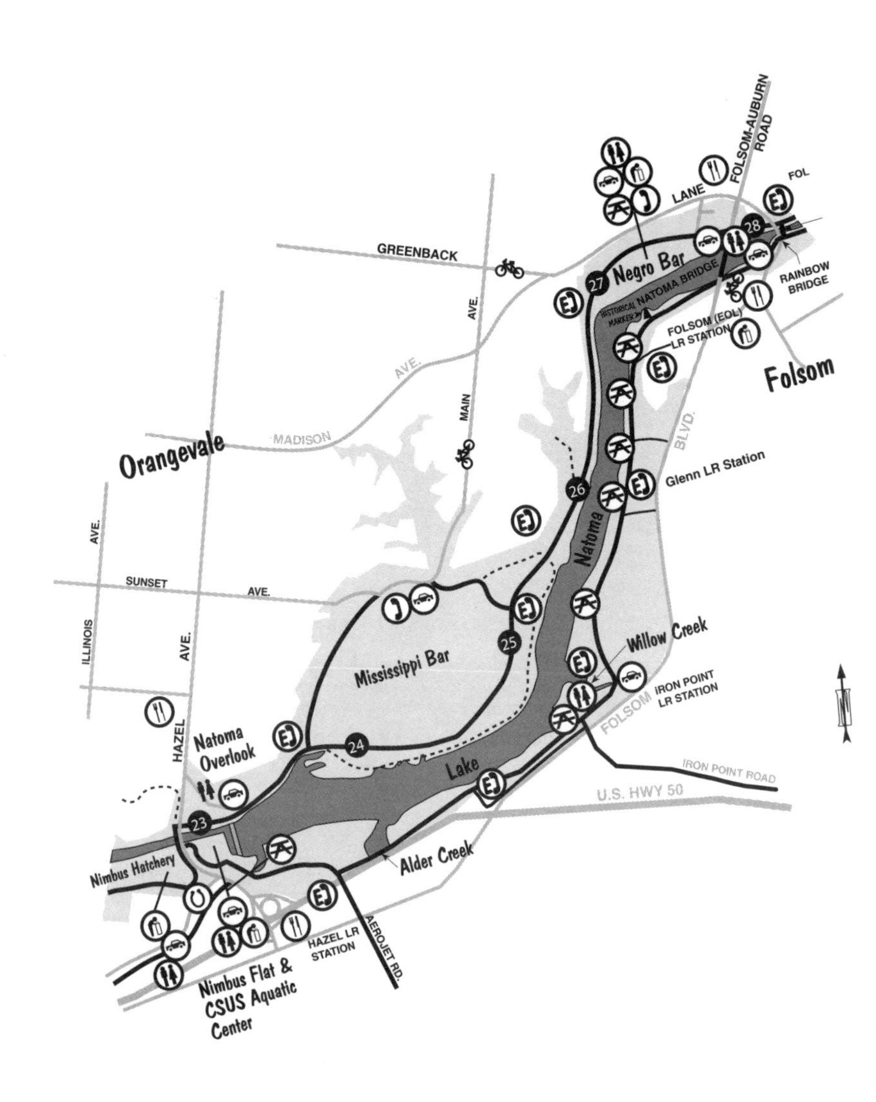

FOLSOM-AUBURN ROAD
FOL
LANE
GREENBACK
Negro Bar
NATOMA BRIDGE
HISTORICAL MARKER
RAINBOW BRIDGE
FOLSOM (EOL) LR STATION
Folsom
AVE.
MAIN
MADISON
AVE.
BLVD.
Orangevale
Glenn LR Station
Natoma
ILLINOIS
AVE.
SUNSET
AVE.
HAZEL
AVE.
Mississippi Bar
Willow Creek
IRON POINT LR STATION
FOLSOM
Natoma Overlook
Lake
IRON POINT ROAD
U.S. HWY 50
Nimbus Hatchery
Alder Creek
HAZEL LR STATION
AEROJET RD.
Nimbus Flat & CSUS Aquatic Center
23
24
25
26
27
28

Hazel Avenue to Rainbow Bridge

Miles 23–28.3

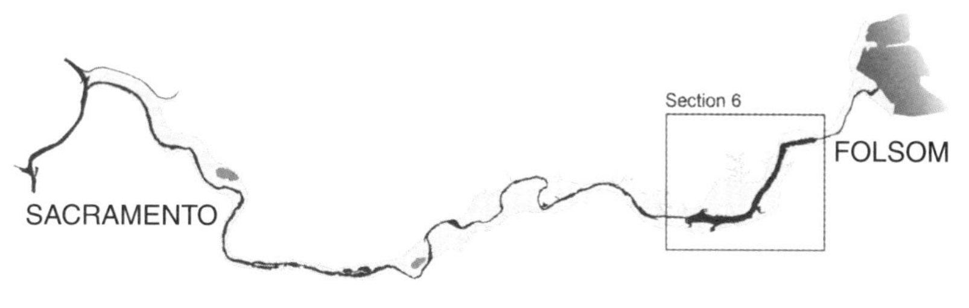

To reach the bicycle trail from the north side of **Hazel Avenue Bridge** travel down the dirt path on the west side of the bridge or the staired ramp on the east. Parking for this access is at Natoma Overlook reached off Hazel Avenue, northeast of the bridge.

The last nine miles of the American River Parkway are part of the Folsom Lake State Recreation Area. Along the 5.3 miles of trail from Hazel Avenue to Rainbow Bridge you can see geological evidence of a distant past–a tale of ancient seas and rivers. Historically, this section is also a rich area–the Natoma Company, Mississippi Bar, Orangevale, Negro Bar and the town of Folsom provide many stories. Rainbow Bridge is about the same elevation as Hazel Avenue, but the plants along the undulating trail are beginning to reflect their location near the foothills. State Park picnic area, boat launching facilities, campgrounds and facilities along Lake Natoma and Folsom Lake attract visitors from throughout California.

Natoma Overlook offers a spectacular view of the surrounding area. West of the parking area, rare vernal pools and spring wildflowers such as larkspur, goldfield, popcorn flower, downingia, brodiaea, and mariposa lily make this location a good place to begin your trip. Vernal pools only have water a few weeks each year, but during that time they teem with life. As the pools evaporate, different plants bloom at the water's edge.

White-throated swifts make their nests under Hazel Avenue Bridge in spring. They often soar high in their search for insects. These swifts have long pointed wings and are black with tuxedo–like black and white fronts.

MILE 23

Mile 23 is where the staired Hazel Avenue access meets the trail under some majestic blue oak trees. Blue oaks populate foothill slopes and are recognized from a distance by their bluish hue.

As you move past the State Park mileage sign, in spring the bright orange blossoms of California poppy, the state's official flower, dot nearby hillsides and fields. It's easy to see why Spanish explorers called this beautiful flower *copa de oro*, cup of gold. Indian legend suggests that the gold in California came from the poppy's fallen petals.

During the salmon run in fall and winter, you may see many fishermen trying their luck at the river below Nimbus Dam and power plant. The fish that made it past the hatchery will not be able to spawn. They have ended up in a dead–end pool with no riffles or gravel beds.

A bicyclist takes in the view of Nimbus dam and the line of fisherman trying their luck.

ROBIN DONNELLY

Nimbus Dam was built in 1955, at the same time as Folsom Dam. It created **Lake Natoma**, an afterbay which provides extra control of Folsom's outflow into the American River. Folsom Lake and Lake Natoma provide acres of water and shoreline for recreation and wildlife habitat.

As you round the Nimbus power plant, look at the bluffs above you. They are part of the **Mehrten Formation**, a series of volcanic mudflows millions of years old. They originated on the east side of what is now the Sierra Nevada before the mountains were lifted by faulting. A strip of cobbled granite, part of an ancient river bed, runs along the cliff. These cobble deposits were left by fast river flows. The sand layers were laid down during slower flows.

Lake *Natoma* (from the Nisenan words *nuto* for east and *mon* for water) was named after the Natoma Company, a pivotal company in the development of the Sacramento area and the American River Parkway.

The Natoma Company

Founded in 1851, the ***Natoma Company*** *soon brought water for mining from a dam at Salmon Falls to outlying areas through miles of pipes, reservoirs, and canals. By 1863, the company became involved in the development of power, irrigation, lumber, and agriculture. When phylloxera disease wiped out the extensive vineyards in 1906, the company switched its attention to gold dredging in the rich lands bordering the American River. By 1910, it owned 30,000 acres of the Leidesdorff Mexican land grant and was so large its stock was traded on the New York Stock Exchange. When dredgers clanked to a halt in 1962, most of the company's holdings were slowly converted to commercial and residential development. In the 1960s and 70s, the Natoma Company's cooperation with the County provided vital acres for the expansion of the American River Parkway. You can still visit the old winery buildings at Nimbus off Hazel Ave and Highway 50.*

Near **Mile 23.8** a dirt and gravel road skirts the western edge of **Mississippi Bar** and ends at **Sunset Avenue**. Until recently, the Teichert Company operated a huge gravel mining operation near the upper end of the road. Most gravel operations in the Sacramento region also produce gold. The land in this area will be reclaimed and returned to the Parkway. The road and the hiking trails leading into this fascinating area make Mississippi Bar easy to explore.

Mississippi Bar in the 1850s

Mississippi Bar *was named by a fur trader from Mississippi who established an Indian trading post here. It became a booming camp of several hundred miners early in the gold rush. Lucky miners shared small cabins at the bend of the dusty stretch of road here. Beginning in 1854, the American River Ditch, also known as the North Fork Ditch or Mississipi Bar Ditch, funneled water from 39 miles upriver to the lower American River gold fields. Gold dredging began here in late 1898. Greaves ferry crossed the river near here and connected to the Old Coloma road.*

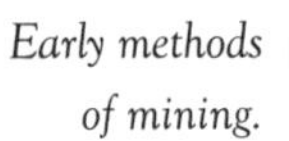

Early methods of mining.

FOLSOM HISTORY MUSEUM

After you cross the culvert, several good trails in the next 0.5 Miles lead into an important wetlands area.

MILE 24

Wetlands

Wetlands *are the birthplace of rivers and seas and harbor a great variety of life. Look for water striders patrolling the surface, crayfish scuttling along the silt bottom, and catfish and mosquito fish hiding among roots of tule and cattail. Birds find cover and make nests in the cattail's fibrous stalks. Frogs, fish, and insects find shelter for their eggs and*

young, making shore areas like these a rich feeding place for many creatures.

Cattails *have a brown flower spike which make them easy to identify during summer and fall. Nisenan roasted early spring's green, pencil–thick flower head and peeled tender cattail roots and stems and ate them raw. The brown head is packed with seeds which provided downy material used by Nisenan for diapering. Even if a hungry muskrat finds and disrupts the cattails nutrient rich underwater rhizomes, remnants just float to a new location and take root again. Muskrats use their webbed hind feet and vertically flattened tail to swim through wetlands, feeding on plants and freshwater clams and crayfish.*

Visiting this area at dusk, you would hear a symphony. Red–winged black birds, and little gray–black coots are regaling you with their chatter. Coots are a marsh bird (not a duck) with lobed, not webbed feet. Diving, they reach depths up to 25 feet in search of leaves, seeds, and roots, then bob back up tail first.

Another inhabitant in this wetland world is the bullfrog. Bullfrogs are the largest frog in North America with a body up to eight inches long and hind legs up to ten inches long. Their coloring is olive–green with yellow to whitish undersides. With the help of their sticky long tongues and large mouths, **bullfrogs** *catch insects, earthworms, snails, small fish, small mammals, and even small birds.*

Perhaps you can also catch a glimpse of a pied–billed grebe here. This gray–brown diving bird has a black throat patch and a dark ring around its bill. In spring, keep on the lookout for a nest floating in decaying vegetation. Grebes use the heat from decay to help keep their eggs warm. Diving birds often have razor–sharp, serrated bills–the better to catch and eat fish. Their smaller wings are streamlined underwater but not as powerful when flying, especially when taking off.

Killdeer, robin–sized birds you might also see or hear near this wetland, have a black–banded white chest, buffy rump patch and familiar call, "kill dee, kill dee." The nest is a depression on pebbly shores with the eggs resembling rounded pebbles. A female killdeer often fakes a broken wing to distract a predator from her nest.

By **Mile 24.5** the trail begins to move away from the Lake. The prevalence of bush monkey flowers, gray pine trees, and toyon shrubs gives the area a feel of the foothills.

Near **Mile 24.8** a 0.15 mile side trail leads to the lake.

"It is a good thing...to make short excursions now and then...to learn something of what is going on in those out of the way places...."– John Muir

RANDY SMITH

Lake Natoma Shore

Travel on the dirt trail, cross the equestrian trail and continue to the lake's edge. A grassy knoll next to the lake is great for picnicking. Pines, oaks, buckbrush, and in the spring and summer, pipevine swallowtail butterflies, wildflowers, and soap plant help make this spot a special find. Soap plant's long wavy blue-green leaves spread on the ground. A tall stout stem with small white star-like flowers appears as summer approaches. Nisenan used the young leaf shoots and bulb as food and the fibrous covering of the bulb as a brush.

Across the lake and west is ***Alder Creek****. Up this creek an active placer mining site of the same name existed in the early days of the gold rush. Beyond Alder Creek was Prairie City, a gold mining town on the Natoma Company's canal. It was once a railroad stop and mining town of nearly 2,000 people.*

To the southeast is ***Willow Creek****, an important wetlands and recreation area. The creek runs by the site of the old town of Natoma. The town was once known as Dredge because of its large dredge repair facilities. It was owned by the Armour Company of meat packing fame. Because the company used the color yellow extensively on their buildings, including employee housing, those who lived there were called "Yellow Town Kids."*

Near **Mile 25** you begin to get the flavor of the area a hundred years ago when dredgers made these hills of tailings. Gold dredging was once so lucrative even foreign companies owned dredgers along the American River.

You can get to the hilltop, a good place for a picnic with a view, by walking on any of the trails in the next 0.2 miles.

Near **Mile 25.5** is the half-mile route to **Main Avenue** in Orangevale. A riding stable is located up this trail near Sunset Avenue.

Cottonwood and willow trees take advantage of the moisture from the many drainage ditches around here. These ditches may be the remnants of the water system established in gold mining days. Old mining ditches brought water to fledgling colonies like Orange Vale.

Orange Vale

Orange Vale *was the second colony established on the San Juan land grant in 1844. Settlers were encouraged to purchase ten acre tracts for $1,250. It was advertised that a family could sustain itself with six acres planted in orchards, two in grapes, with the remaining two in buildings and alfalfa.*

One of the most intriguing settlers in Orange Vale was **John Cardwell***. After clearing the land, he purchased the 80–foot steamship,* Daisy, *and rigged up a barge behind her to haul cords of wood to Sacramento. Bridges, river snags and low water proved too difficult for the ship. When Cardwell's huge woodpile caught fire, the project ended–as did the last attempt to use steamers to navigate the American River.*

Between **Miles 25.5** and **26** toyon shrubs decorate the hillside. This large shrub has dark evergreen leaves which are lighter underneath. The white flowers of spring and summer become bright red berries in winter, a feast for birds such as robins, mockingbirds and cedar waxwings. Cedar waxwings have a black face mask, pointed crest, yellow tail trim and bright red tips on the wing feathers which look like they were dipped in red wax. Known as the gentlemen of the bird world, they often share food with companions.

Horehound is a common useful plant in this area. It grows in clumps one to three feet high. The gray–green wrinkled leaves were used for the treatment of colds and high blood pressure. Horehound candy is still a remedy you can try today.

At **Mile 26** the trail makes a downhill run into the coolness by Lake Natoma.

If you want to see what this area looked like before the invasion of star thistle, hike up to **Snipes Ravine**.

Take the dirt trail which is just past the pond. Walk up the hill, then keep veering left up the ravine about half a mile to an old rusted truck. Go right on either of the trails up the hill. This park can also be reached off of ***Pershing*** *and* ***Snipes Roads****. These accesses make Snipes Ravine a good starting and ending point for Parkway explorations. Vernal pools, wild flowers, blue oak trees and rare purple needlegrass help make this park a special find.*

As you continue between lake and bluff in spring, look for Clarkia. Its smooth narrow leaves have red veins, and by May and June, crimson flowers spot the hillside. Clarkia was named for William Clark of the Lewis and Clark fame, as was *Clarkia purpurea*, commonly known as farewell-to-spring. This late-bloomer's flowers vary from purple to light pink and can be found up the trail when other plants have turned brown.

A deep crevice with a buckeye tree near Mile 26.6 is a good place to stop to take a closer look at the Mehrten mudflows protruding from the cliff. The mudflows here are spotted with orange and green splotches of crustlike lichen. Lichens are not considered parasitic, but represent a partnership of two different kinds of plants, alga and fungus. The algae make the food, and the fungi provide structure, water storage, and minerals.

In summer and fall, look for California fuchsia's (hummingbird's trumpet) vivid scarlet blossoms. Woolly stems and narrow grayish leaves help protect this plant from the sun's fierce glare.

It would take about 1,000 fuchsia blossoms to feed the tiny Anna's hummingbird. A year–round Parkway resident, its blackish head and throat flash a bright crimson as its feathers catch the light. Hummingbirds move their wings at more than 75 wing beats per second. To maintain such a high metabolism they need to consume their weight in nectar daily. Some hummingbirds are incredible travelers. The tiny rufous hummingbird seen here in fall and spring flies over stormy oceans and steep coastal mountains during its 2,500 mile journey from Alaska to Central America.

As you near **Mile 26.9,** a gray pine tree on the top of the cliff leans over the trail. On the east side of the tree is a small geological fault. It can be identified as a fault because the thick cobble beds are cut off. Barn owls have hollowed out nests here in the weakened rock. These owls have a white face and white underparts flecked with brown. Owls swallow their food whole. What isn't digested is regurgitated as pellets which are often found on the ground near their roost.

Nearby, barn swallow nests look like pueblos attached to the sides of the hill. Barn swallows have long pointed wings, a cinnamon-brown breast, and a deeply forked tail. Don't look for this fast flying, insect-eating bird in winter. They will be long gone to South America.

A hundred feet further along the trail, about 20 feet up the bluff, is a layer of white volcanic ash under the exposures of stream gravels and sand bars. Million of years ago volcanoes erupted where the Sierra now exist, leaving behind many of the rocks and sediments we see today.

Across the lake near the gravel piles was the site of **Texas Hill**. Established in 1849, the town soon petered out as a gold camp but possessed another valuable rock–cobblestones. These cobblestones paved many streets in San Francisco and Sacramento.

Look east for a view of Rainbow Bridge, the gateway to the foothills.

Negro Bar Day Use Area, part of Folsom Lake Recreation Area, begins after **Mile 27** and extends for almost a mile. Extensive picnic facilities, parking and a swimming beach make Negro Bar a convenient place to begin or end your journey on the Parkway. This park is actually situated on Maine Bar.

The site of **Negro Bar** is on the south bank of the American River across from the park. African-Americans began to mine the Bar in 1849. Almost overnight Negro Bar became a community of around 700 people, a racial mix, boasting a hotel, two general stores, a Pony Express stop, a saloon and some women.

Women helped turn the rugged gold mining camps into towns, but differed in opinion as to their lives here. Mary Ballou ran a Negro Bar boarding house. She complained she was up at night scaring hogs and mules out of the house and spent $4 for a chicken and $3 for a dozen eggs. Other women relished the greater opportunities the gold rush provided. While the demands for hotels, cooking and laundry services were great, many women owned businesses and were paid good wages.

An estimated $50 million in gold (at today's prices) came out of Negro Bar, but its fame was short-lived. The easy diggings dried up by 1851 and the town washed away in a flood the following year. Today, most of Negro Bar lies under the waters of Lake Natoma.

William Leidesdorff

Perhaps the best remembered legacy left by a black man in this area is that of the Dutch/West Indian ***William Leidesdorff****. He once owned the land south of the American River from Bradshaw Road to the foothills. He skippered trading voyages between San Francisco and Hawaii, and was successful in many business ventures. Service as a diplomat to Mexico won him the 35,520 acre grant he called Rancho Rio de los Americanos, part of which later became the city of Folsom. In 1848, soon after gold was discovered in Coloma, Leidesdorff visited the grant, but died of a fever a couple weeks later at his home in San Francisco.*

After **Mile 27**, begin your climb toward the foothills. You are rising out of the fifty million year old Ione sea bed that once covered the Sacramento Valley. Waters of the Ione Sea swarmed with marine dinosaurs such as forty-foot plesiosaurs and fifty-foot mosasaurs. A throwback to the dinosaur age with a pedigree seventy million years old, sturgeon found in the American River today can grow up to twenty feet long, weigh hundreds of pounds, and live for a hundred years.

In the next mile are many Negro Bar facilities. The new **Lake Natoma American River Bridge** passes over the bicycle trail and join with Greenback Lane and Auburn-Folsom Road.

Folsom Powerhouse

Descend on the trail to the parking lot at the river's edge near ***Mile 28.2****. This is a good place to see river boulders and appreciate the force with which the American River carves and polishes granite. The low lying rocks across the river have holes where Nisenan once ground acorns. Not long after the last vestiges of acorn meal were swept from the rock, the* **Folsom Powerhouse State Historic Park,** *across Lake Natoma, on top of the river bank, transmitted the first public long distance electrical power in the world. It was built by the Folsom Water Power Company run by Horatio Livermore Jr. of the Natoma Water and Mining Company. On July 13, 1895 copper wires stretched twenty–two miles to a substation at 6th and H Streets, lighting up Sacramento. The company sold the powerhouse in 1903 to what would become the Pacific Gas and Electric Company.*

The town of **Folsom** has a lively history. With William Leidesdorff barely cold in his grave, **Captain Joseph Folsom** wrangled an appointment as estate executor and traveled to see Leidesdorff's mother and heir in the West Indies. There he bought Rancho Rio de los Americanos and Leidesdorff's extensive San Francisco holdings for $75,000. When Leidesdorff's relatives realized the true value of the estate they filed a lawsuit, but were thwarted by an 1850 law which forbade Negroes from suing whites.

The **Sacramento Valley Railroad (SVRR)** began service on February 22, 1856. It carried 1,000 people on free excursions to Folsom for champagne and partying which lasted through the night. The completion of the railroad placed the town of Folsom as the pivotal link between the riverboats coming into Sacramento and the mining camps in the foothills. More than twenty stage lines were centered in Folsom and scheduled their departures shortly after the arrival of the train from Sacramento. In July 1860, the SVRR carried mail from the Pony Express station in Folsom down to Sacramento.

Folsom is a fascinating historic town with museums, shops and restaurants, and a new network of hiking and biking trails.

Folsom

Cross Rainbow Bridge using the elevated path on the east side. (After the pedestrian bridge is in place, use it instead.) First visit the old powerhouse just west of the bridge. (Tours are provided Wednesday through Sunday afternoons, call (916) 985-4843 for times.) There is a Nisenan grinding hole site below the Powerhouse on the river's edge. The Chamber of Commerce is in the historic railroad depot area. Here you can pick up information and a map of the town. Nearby is the original 1868 Ashland Freight Depot. Walk up toward the Wells Fargo Building and the ***Folsom History Museum*** *at 823 Sutter Street. If you go to the museum's backyard you can see where spring water still bubbles out of the earth. Water from this spring was once enjoyed by the horses of the Pony Express when they stabled here. Visit Sturm's Hotel where it is said ghosts still reside, or work your way up Scott Street past Folsom's "Nob Hill" of Victorian houses. The Chinese and Pioneer Cemeteries, off Folsom Boulevard, are an easy bicycle ride away. Surveying the grave markers in Folsom's old cemeteries is a reminder that many people died before the age of 40.*

A network of trails is just east of Rainbow Bridge. A paved bicycle lane leads up to the Folsom City Park, the Folsom Rodeo Grounds and the Folsom City Zoo. Dirt hiking trails take advantage of the terrain closer to the river and offer spectacular river views. The main trail runs toward Folsom Prison alongside the original canal built for the Folsom Powerhouse.

East Lake Natoma Trail

Another premier trail option for hiking or biking is the East Lake Natoma hiking, biking, and equestrian trail that joins with the Jedediah Smith Bicycle Trail at Hazel Avenue. Cross Riley to Leidsdorff Street to the trail entrance east of the Lake Natoma Bridge.

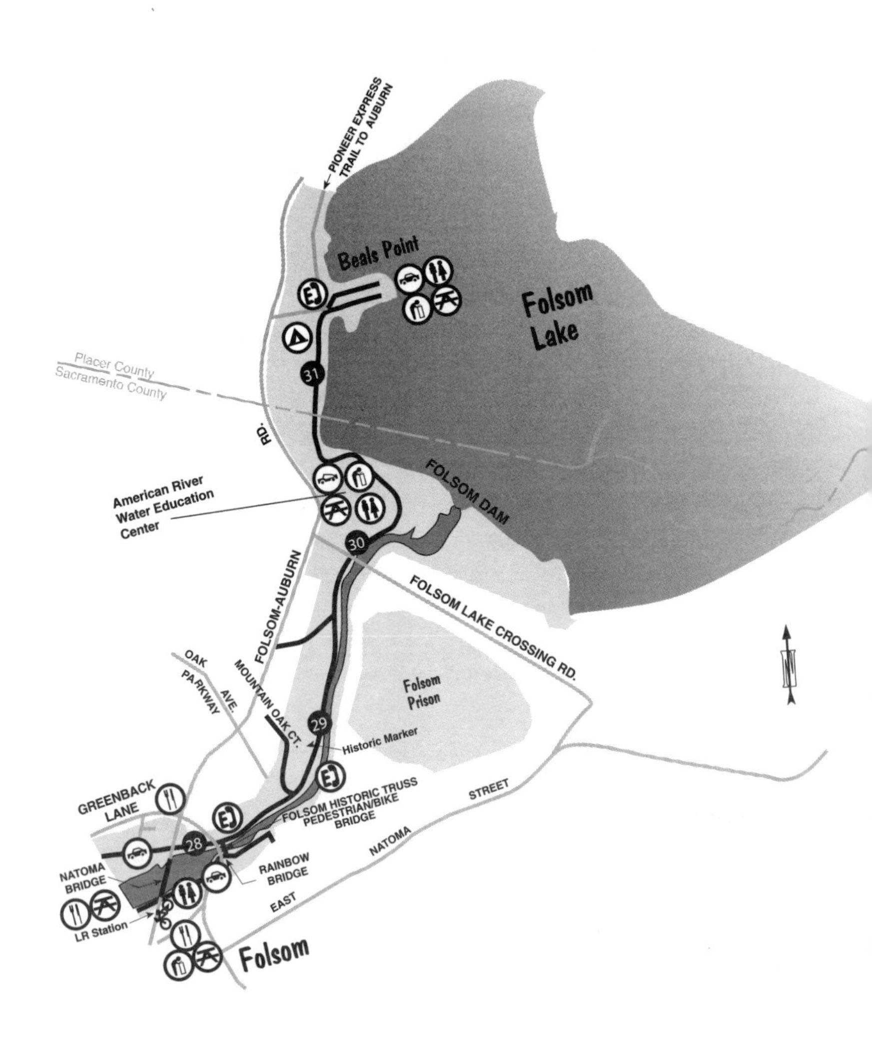PIONEER EXPRESS TRAIL TO AUBURN
Beals Point
Folsom Lake
Placer County
Sacramento County
31
RD.
FOLSOM DAM
American River Water Education Center
30
FOLSOM-AUBURN
FOLSOM LAKE CROSSING RD.
OAK
PARKWAY
AVE.
MOUNTAIN OAK CT.
Folsom Prison
29
Historic Marker
GREENBACK LANE
FOLSOM HISTORIC TRUSS PEDESTRIAN/BIKE BRIDGE
STREET
NATOMA
28
NATOMA BRIDGE
RAINBOW BRIDGE
EAST
LR Station
Folsom

Rainbow Bridge to Beals Point

Miles 28.3–31.6

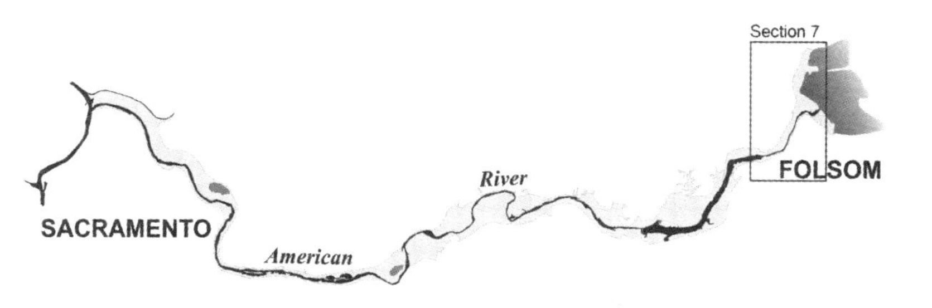

On the upriver side of Rainbow Bridge is the access between the bicycle trail, **Rainbow Bridge**, **Greenback Lane**, and the **Folsom Historic Truss Bridge**.

As you travel the 3.3 miles between Rainbow Bridge and Beals Point the terrain becomes more rugged and there are spectacular views looking down into the American River Canyon, across to Folsom Prison, and finally, out to Folsom Lake. You will be climbing almost 300 feet in elevation. Species of plants more typical of the foothills such as gray pine trees, buck brush, yerba santa and manzanita will be more common. This section is a fascinating part of the Parkway and is well-worth the climb. In fact, the climb is part of the fun, especially when you keep in mind the great downhill reward on the return trip.

At **Mile 28.3** look back at **Rainbow Bridge**, the only arch bridge in Sacramento County. Completed in 1917, this busy bridge handles an estimated thirty to forty thousand cars a day. Getting across the river has never been an easy matter. Water draining from foothills and mountains rages through the American River canyon here.

The **Folsom Historic Truss Bridge** creates an important link to Folsom and bicycle and pedestrian trails to the southeast of the Jedediah Smith Bicycle Trail. The first two Folsom bridges were swept away in floods and a third bridge's cable snapped, dropping the bridge into the river. In 1893 a replacement one–lane steel truss bridge finally opened. It served traffic until the two–laned Rainbow Bridge made it obsolete. Taken apart in 1931, the sturdy bridge was reassembled in Siskiyou County crossing the Klamath River. It is now being moved back to this site for pedestrian and bicycle traffic. The **California Central Railroad Bridge** once crossed the river at the site of Rainbow Bridge. The railroad was headquartered in Ashland the junction of Folsom-Auburn Road and Greenback Lane.

California Central Railroad Bridge

PHOTO COURTESY FOLSOM HISTORICAL MUSEUM

Off Greenback Lane is Folsom-Auburn Road, an early stagecoach route which once wound even closer to the bicycle trail. Outlaw gangs once hid in these hills, preying upon the stages which serviced the gold mining towns. One gang stole 40 pounds of gold which is reputed to be buried in the area.

Before you head up the trail, pay attention to the sign about **mountain lions**. Though it is unusual to catch a glimpse of one of these solitary and beautiful creatures, as both human and mountain lion populations have increased, more sightings and confrontations occur. Mountain lions (cougars) are yellowish to reddish brown in color with a long heavy tail. A male can weigh up to 180 pounds, a female up to 130 pounds. Mountain lions usually hunt alone at night. In California, wherever you find deer, coyote, rabbits and other small mammals, you might also find this stealthy predator.

In the unlikely event that you ever come face to face with a lion, act big. Raise your arms, open your jacket, pick up small children—don't run. Most lions will be as afraid of you as you are of them.

In the spring and summer, poppy, vetch, bush monkey flower and lupine mix in with buck brush and yerba santa. Buck brush is an evergreen shrub with small, wedge-shaped, leathery leaves which are well-adapted to arid or chaparral conditions. White clusters of flowers make their appearance from March to May. When buck brush seeds are ripe, the capsules explode under the hot summer sun, sending seeds flying in the air. If you sit quietly, you can actually hear the capsules burst. Buck brush often appears in foothill areas which have been burned, providing important feed for deer after other vegetation has been destroyed.

Fire

The Nisenan were adept at the careful use of fire to replenish the land, control dense undergrowth, or to corral food such as grasshoppers. Many of the fires which presently occur in the Parkway are very damaging because they burn too hot or are uncontrolled.

Yerba santa (mountain balm) is increasingly prevalent as you move up the trail. A perennial shrub found on dry slopes, its resinous, varnished-looking leaves are oblong and tapering with a woolly underside. In May and June, pale lavender funnel-shaped flowers appear in clusters. Its name means "holy plant" in Spanish and refers to the plant's healing powers.

Near **Mile 28.5** is the beginning of **Slate Bar**, a large ledge of slate, schist, and granite overlooking the river. In the early 1850s and 1860s a succession of flour mills here produced up to 50 barrels of superior, reasonably priced flour a day. To the miners and settlers who had suffered through the 1852 Mother Lode famine a local gristmill was the answer to a prayer.

A sidetrip to Slate Bar is rewarding and offers beautiful views of the river canyon.

Slate Bar

Just after the trail bend near Mile 28.5, take the small dirt road leading into Slate Bar. The river pouring through the canyon here once turned the mill wheels at ***Stockton's Mill****.*

The area is a good place to look for schist, a crystaline rock with many color divisions, and slate, a hardened form of dark gray shale. You'll also find many granite deposits and some riffraff left over from building Folsom Dam. Granite is crystalized magma, a remnant of volcanoes which eventually eroded.

In spring, as you walk toward the river, paintbrush plants poke flower–like red heads up between the rocks. A small trail leading back toward Rainbow Bridge passes by Nisenan grinding holes in the rocks overlooking the river. Sidetrails like this one are only for the hardy and careful hiker.

Just as you see the wall of Folsom Prison near **Mile 28.7** the trail bends northward and climbs toward Folsom Lake. The next half mile, and the last half mile of the trail, are the steadiest inclines. You are climbing up a tilted block fault, the result of a geological process which began about 10 million years ago.

Spanish broom is found along the trail. Despite their sweet–smelling yellow flowers, an effort is underway to remove these invasive shrubs from the Parkway. Household brooms were made by binding the slender rush–like branches together.

MILE 29

At **Mile 29** the **Mountain View Court** overpass offers access to residential neighborhoods and Auburn-Folsom Road. The Parkway is very narrow here and serves as an essential channel for wildlife. There have been several sightings of mountain lions in this vicinity.

Near **Mile 29.2** the stone ruins west of the trail are part of a building that likely dates to the time this was a thriving olive-producing area. The olive trees on the hill date from the late 1800s. Blackberry bushes surround the creek and give a seasonal leafy frame to the ruin's old granite–block doors and windows. The old fig tree in the corner, the nearby stream, berry bushes, and plenty of nesting holes make this rocky ruin a perfect habitat for a raccoon.

Figs are a favorite food of raccoons. Their varied diet also includes fish, shellfish, insects, mice, birds, fruits, berries and acorns. Inquisitive and crafty, they hunt at night, often foraging near creeks or rivers where you can see their long-toed footprints in the soft ground. Their Latin name *lotor*, meaning one who washes, indicates their preference to wash their food before eating.

Near **Mile 29.3** is an access to the **Folsom-Auburn Road** and the equestrian trail. The hiking and equestrian trails between here and Folsom Dam offer good places to view the river, Folsom Prison, the old dam site, and experience nature first-hand.

Granite posts along the bicycle trail are almost hidden amidst the live oak and black locust trees. Made at Folsom Prison, these posts once lined Greenback Lane before it was widened. With the creation of this trail, they were relocated here. As you round the bend after **Mile 29.5**, the chain link fence denotes the boundary of Folsom Prison.

Near **Mile 29.9 fairy lantern (globe lily)** may be found on the rocky bank in the spring and summer. This beautiful lily has several satiny white lantern-like flowers on a single stem. Attractive three-winged seed capsules soon follow. In other moist crevices along upper Parkway trails, careful observers can sometimes find the delicate fan-shaped leaflet of the California maidenhair fern. The shiny black stems of the maidenhair were used by the Nisenan to weave fine designs into baskets. Orientation to the sun causes slopes to have remarkably different vegetation.

A **Folsom Prison** viewpoint is just before **Mile 30** on the rocky bank. The prison was opened in 1880 with almost 100 prisoners. Today it houses around 7,000 inmates. For a closer look at the prison and a history of the first Folsom Dam, pull into the viewpoint marked by the camera sign here.

Prison bicycle race

FOLSOM PRISON MUSEUM

Folsom Prison

*Before **Folsom Prison** opened, San Quentin was the state's only prison. By 1851 it was so severely overcrowded Governor Peter Burnett was recommending the death penalty for grand larceny and robbery. In 1868, Horatio Livermore, head of the Natoma Company, offered the State of California a 350–acre site for a prison in exchange for prison labor to build an American River dam and canal for his company. Folsom Prison officially opened for business in July of 1880, with two cell blocks made from hand-cut granite. Since there were no walls, boundary lines were set by the warden and enforced by sharpshooters. You can still see the original gothic–like building toward the middle of the facility near the river.*

Prison industry was once a big business. Many granite buildings and roads in Sacramento and San Francisco were built of rock cut or crushed by prisoners in Folsom. Beginning in 1894, the prison's ice plant contributed to the development of the fruit growing industry in California, making it possible to ship fruit to markets throughout the United States. The Folsom Prison Museum is off Green Valley Road.

Don't venture into the river canyon as it is Folsom Prison property. To the south of the viewpoint is the site of the first Folsom Dam completed in 1893.

In the early 1850s, **Horatio Livermore** saw the river raging through Stony Bar Gorge, just upriver from Folsom Prison, and envisoned an industrial city energized by dam water diverted though canals to spin sawmill and factory wheels. In 1893 his sons succeeded in completing the dam and canal. By then a more innovative dam system could be used to generate electricity in powerplants instead of merely turning wheels in local mills. The granite dam backed up water for four miles. The first fish ladder in the state ran up one side. The dam was dynamited in the 1950s during construction of the present Folsom Dam. You can see remnants more easily by taking a short sidetrip.

Old Folsom Dam

Walk on the small dirt trail found midway between the bicycle trail and the prison viewpoint. Go south 0.2 mile to a large granite boulder where you can see dam ruins near the northwest wall of the prison. During one storm in the 1890s, a log boom broke causing three million feet of logs stored for the Folsom sawmill to sweep over the dam and be scattered as far as Rio Vista. You will notice the ruins are above the existing bed of the American River. The river bed was lowered to allow more power generation when the new Folsom Dam was built in 1955.

Old Folsom Dam

PHOTO COURTESY FOLSOM HISTORICAL MUSEUM

At **Mile 30.25** you can visit the **American River Water Education Center.**

After the underpass is an access to **Folsom Lake Crossing**, a four-lane span with an off-street bicycle and pedestrian trail. Opened in 2009, is is just downstream from Folsom Dam, which is closed to all traffic, and links Folsom-Auburn Road and East Natomas Street in Folsom.

Folsom Dam

***Folsom Dam** is a water storage and hydro–electric project completed as part of the Central Valley Project in 1955. The amount of cement used to build the dam was enough to build a sidewalk three feet wide from San Francisco to New York. Folsom is by far the biggest of the 20 existing dams in the American River watershed. Upon completion, instead of a predicted three years to fill the dam, a combination of snow melt and torrential rains brought it to capacity in eight days.*

In July of 1995, failure of the Number 3 gate caused water from a brimming Folsom Lake to rush downstream. New improvements in dam maintanence and downstream levees, as well as flood planning using current upstream dams and downstream runoff channels, help protect the 350,000 people who live in the Sacramento area flood plain. An ongoing difficult task at Folsom Dam is deciding how much water to release to offset salinity in the Sacramento River Delta, meet domestic and valley irrigation demands, and keep enough water in the American River to maintain fisheries and recreation.

Up the trail, near **Mile 30.7** is the **San Juan Water Treatment Facility** which supplies water to both Placer and Sacramento counties.

At **Mile 31** gray pine, live and blue oak trees, coffeeberry and man root prevail. California man root (wild cucumber) is a climbing vine that can grow to 30 feet long. The tips of their curly tendrils are touch–sensitive. When they contact a support they curl around it in a matter of hours. Man root's large dark seeds, a product of the round green, spiny, poisonous fruit, were used by Spanish–Californian children for marbles and by native people as beads. Crushing the seeds also provided Nisenan with hair cream.

Conifers like the gray pine have conical shapes to allow sun to reach their lower branches and to lower wind resistance. They are one of the plants that grow different types of leaves depending on how much sunlight is available. Conifer saplings can start out with larger "shade needles" and switch to "sun needles" when they've broken through the surrounding canopy of vegetation.

At **Mile 31.1** is one of the **Folsom Lake State Recreation Area** campgrounds. A striking specimen of common (or Parry) manzanita is trailside. Its beautiful smooth red bark peels as it grows. Pinkish flowers are followed by berries that turn red in fall. Many native tribes celebrated the ripening of the edible berries with a big feast and dance. Birds, ground squirrels and raccoons also eat the berries.

Wild turkeys can sometimes be seen wandering in many parts of the Parkway, seemingly unbothered by human presence. These powerful birds can fly up to fifty miles an hour and run twelve miles an hour on the ground. They have longer legs and necks and are more brilliantly colored than domesticated turkeys. Some native tribes considered turkeys unfit to eat. Benjamin Franklin once proposed the wily wild turkey for our national bird instead of the bald eagle.

Begin your last ascent to Folsom Lake.

At the top of the grade, you are immediately rewarded with an expansive view of Folsom Lake and on clear days, the Sierra Nevada. Numerous campgrounds, picnic areas and trails help make **Folsom Lake** one of California's most popular state recreation areas. The 10,000-acre lake offers swimming, fishing, boating and more than seventy-five miles of shoreline. The snack bar is seasonal.

The **Pioneer Express Trail**, an equestrian and hiking trail to Auburn, begins just up the trail. Bicycles are allowed as far as Granite Bay.

*To reach the **Pioneer Express Trail**, cross the Beals Point access road and start down a small hill. At the trail fork, bend left. This popular trail leads along the northwest edge of Folsom Lake and the North Fork of the American River to Auburn. As you continue up the trail you'll notice islands in the lake which provide an autumn resting stop for hundreds of migrating Canada Geese. The trail ends near the proposed Auburn Dam.*

To complete your journey of the American River Parkway, cross the Beals Point access road, and start down the small incline. When the trail forks, take the paved trail into Beals Point. Travel to the farthest picnic table on the little hill at the point, or, to one of the beach front tables. When the waters of the reservoir rose in 1955, a new world was created, and an old world was lost. Inundated were time-mellowed ranches and wineries, buckeye and oak dotted hills and valleys, and miles of green, cool riverbank.

Beals Point

Beals Point *at* ***Mile 31.6*** *began as a gold mining camp founded by Henry Beals. Though it was not a particularly rich strike, nearby* ***Mormon Island*** *was the second most important gold strike in California. Founded by Mormons in 1848 at the intersection of the North and South Forks of the American River, the town once had a population of 2,500. When Mormon church leader, Brigham Young, asked for a tithe for the Lord from the rich strike, ex-Mormon Sam Brannan (who would eventually die penniless) said he'd be glad to turn over the money if the Lord would sign the receipt. When the reservoir is low, ruins can be seen.*

You have journeyed from an area which was a floodplain for millions of years, and you have seen evidence of a rich geologic past and a gold rush which caused one of the largest migrations known to man. You have learned about interrelationships between plants and animals, and between natives, explorers, miners, settlers and ourselves. If you have managed to make some new friends along the way, whether two-legged or otherwise, then your journey along these trails has not come to an end, but has just begun.

By becoming adept at reading nature's signs, the land becomes more and more your home, and its inhabitants your neighbors.

Appendix

A Tour of Old Sacramento

Begin your journey at the north end of Old Sacramento in front of the **Sacramento Discovery Museum** at 101 I Street. The museum is a replica of the first City Hall and Water Works building. One of its exhibits is a gold display worth a million dollars. You are near the railroad and the river, a fitting place to start. A city grew here because Sacramento was close to the American River gold mines.

Between the Discovery Museum and the Railroad Museum is the **Big Four Building**, which includes the restoration of the original Huntington and Hopkins Hardware store. In the 1850s and '60s supplies for miners and the railroad passed like a river through this store. To the west is the store used by Leland Stanford when he was a grocer. He became a member of the "Big Four" Central Pacific Railroad monopoly with Huntington, Hopkins, and a former brawny blacksmith, Charles Crocker. The offices of the Big Four were located on the second story. It was there the brilliant young engineer, Theodore Judah, presented his daring plan for a transcontinental railroad that would one day become the Central Pacific Railroad.

You can see some of the trains that helped shape a continent by visiting the **State Railroad Museum**, next door at 111 I Street, one of the largest railroad museums in the world.

The Sacramento Railroad Depot was a hub of activity in early Sacramento.

PHOTO COMPLIMENTS OF THE DEYOUNG MUSEUM.

Notice the big dip in the green grassy area across from these museums. This is the pre-1860s level of Sacramento which was flooded again and again in the early 1850s before pioneers began to build levees. These early levees failed, so the whole town was raised by adding cartloads of fill around the buildings. Many underground passages still remain beneath the streets of Old Sacramento as streets were covered over and first floors became basements and new second stories were added.

When considering the magnitude of the early floods in Sacramento, it is no wonder in 1862 *The San Francisco Morning Call* reported, "It is simply an act of folly for the people of Sacramento to endeavor to maintain their city in its present location."

Continue toward J Street past the **Pony Express Statue** and plaques on the east side of 2nd Street. Old Sacramento is a city associated with many firsts:

- Home to the first Western railroad and stage coach line
- Terminus of the first Pony Express ride and telegraph
- Origin of the first transcontinental railroad
- Recipient of the first long distance electric transmission.

The **B. F. Hastings Building,** diagonally across the street on 2nd and J Streets, figured prominently in this early history.

Walk down 2nd toward K Street past the interpretative photos of Old Sacramento. Turn right on K Street toward the Sacramento River. The **Lady Adams Hotel**, 119 K Street, was one of the only buildings south of J Street to survive the fire of 1852. It was built from the non-combustible ballast that had helped a ship of the same name sail around the Horn to Sacramento.

Only a month after the fire of '52, Sacramentans raised an incredible 761 new buildings, including several new hotels. One early observer remarked about "the dozens of miserable, filthy hotels" of the time. "Blankets, which have never been submitted to any cleaning process, are provided for the guests to sleep on...a single washpan answers for all, and one towel, redolent of a week's wiping, serves every guest." Hilton R. Helper *Sacramento* William Holden

Continue down K Street to Front Street. Try walking on the cobblestones. Called Folsom potatoes, they were a huge improvement over the original streets of dust and mud.

A stern wheeler rests at the dock, and remnants of old wharves mark the banks up and down the Sacramento River. The **Delta King** was one of the last paddlewheelers to operate between Sacramento and San Francisco. Launched in 1927, it conveyed passengers in style on its nightly run between the two cities, serving as a floating "gambling" house in the prohibition of the 1930s. Used as a barracks and wounded-soldier transport during World War II, it was later a construction workers' dorm in Alaska.

STAN GARVEY/KING AND QUEEN OF THE RIVER

Half-sunk Delta King in Richmond, California, April 1981, before restoration.

Notice the levee that helps keep the Sacramento River within its channel. Hardin Bigelow was among the first to envision the levee system, and in 1850 he persisted with shovel and grit until others joined him. Credited with saving the city (for the time being anyway), he was named Sacramento's first mayor. He was shot and killed in the same year while trying to prevent a riot over "squatters' rights." After the city was raised and levee improvements were completed in 1873, this downtown area never had another significant flood.

The **Old Sacramento Schoolhouse** is one block south on Front Street.

At the foot of K Street is the **Central Pacific Freight Depot**, and to the north is the passenger station. Here on January 8, 1863, the first spade of earth was turned for the Central Pacific Railroad (CPRR). The street was so muddy a cart-load of soil had to be brought in for the ceremony. Six and a half grueling years later, on May 10, 1869, the rails begun here would connect with the westbound Union Pacific Railroad at Promontory Point, Utah. Theodore Judah began the CPRR after he engineered the Sacramento Valley Railroad (SVRR), the first major railroad west of the Mississippi which began from a depot here in 1856.

Now the depot is again a hub of activity, housing a lively **Public Market** which offers a wide variety of goods and produce.

As you walk north on Front Street, take a look at the roof of the **Newton Booth Building** on the east side of the street. From that raised platform back in the frantic gold rush days, the enterprising Mr. Booth used flags to communicate with ships coming up the river. He then knew what the ships carried and had the goods bought before the ships touched the wharf. In this way Booth gained control of many of the Sacramento bound supplies which were not already purchased by Huntington, Hopkins and Stanford.

Visit the restaurant in the **Brannan Building** on the corner of Front and J Streets to see the ornate rosewood and mahogany bar. This massive structure was carved in France around 1870. It was then shipped around the Horn to Leadville, Colorado, where it stayed until transported here. Tending this bar for thirsty Colorado miners with a need to lubricate their tonsils was how the infamous Molly Brown (*The Unsinkable Molly Brown*) got her start. Sacramento had its own fair share of saloons. Mark Twain, who once wrote for the old *Sacramento Union*, commented, "You can shut your eyes and march into the first door you come to and call for a drink, and the chances are that you will get it."

Cross J Street and continue walking up Front Street to the **Eagle Theatre,** a restoration of what is known as California's first theatre. Originally built in 1849 of wood and canvas with an earth floor, it was a popular distraction for miners. Just north is the site of the **City Hotel,** a showpiece built by Sam Brannan out of the lumber and materials from Captain Sutter's unfinished grist mill. The enterprising Brannan became California's first millionaire, but he died penniless.

Downtown Sacramento

Other downtown bicycling or hiking side trips include the beautifully restored California State Capital Building and Park at 10th between L and N Streets, the Leland and Jane Stanford home at 8th and N Streets, the Crocker Art Museum at 3rd and 0 Streets, and the Old Sacramento City Cemetery at 9th and Broadway (where the history of old Sacramentans is "laid out" amid the quaint and unusual tombstones). Sutter's Fort and the State Indian Museum at 27th and L Street also beckon visitors of all ages.

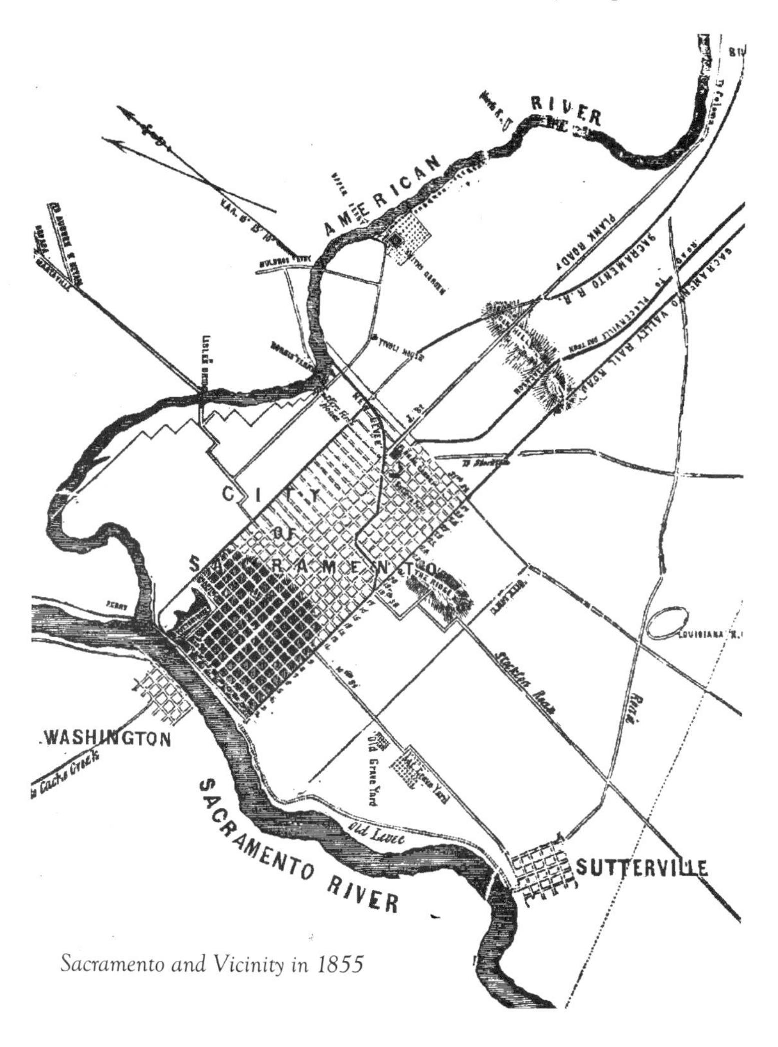

Sacramento and Vicinity in 1855

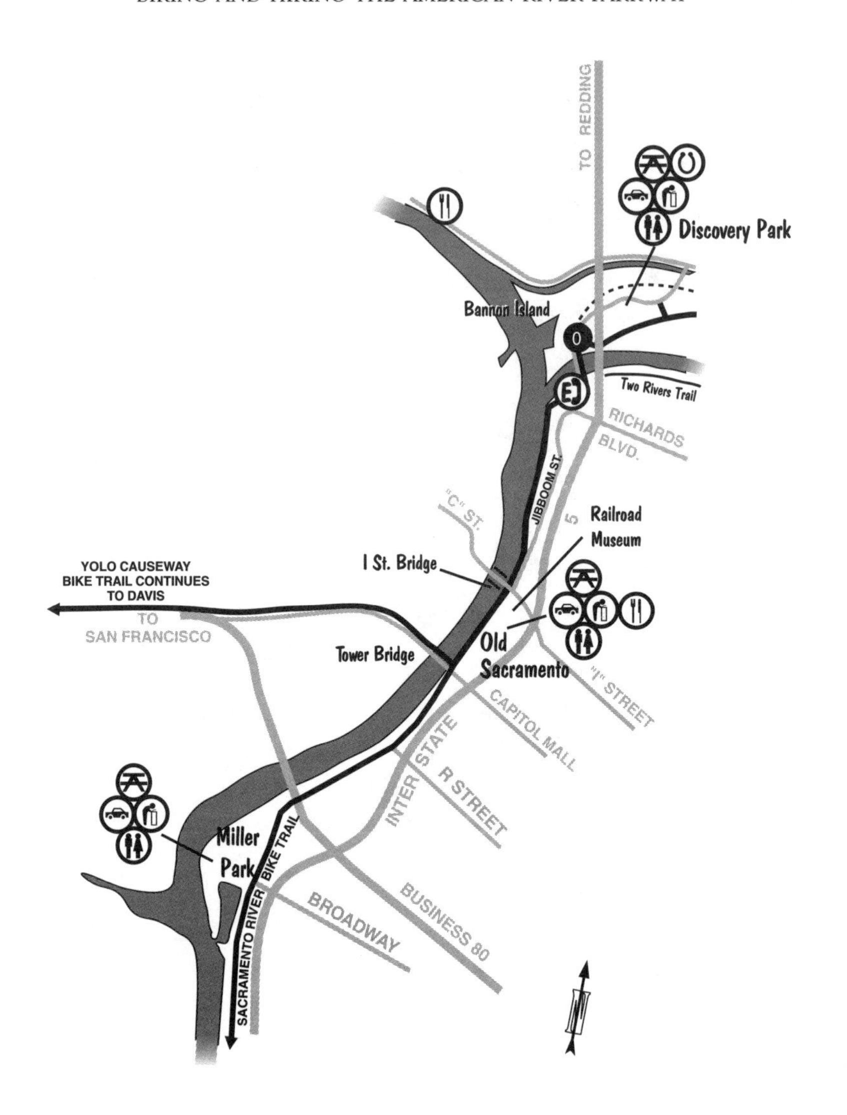
TO REDDING
Discovery Park
Bannon Island
0
EJ
Two Rivers Trail
RICHARDS
BLVD.
JIBBOOM ST.
"C" ST.
5
Railroad
Museum
I St. Bridge
YOLO CAUSEWAY
BIKE TRAIL CONTINUES
TO DAVIS
TO
SAN FRANCISCO
Old
Sacramento
Tower Bridge
"I" STREET
CAPITOL MALL
INTER STATE
R STREET
Miller
Park
SACRAMENTO RIVER BIKE TRAIL
BROADWAY
BUSINESS 80
N

THE SACRAMENTO RIVER BICYCLE TRAIL—1 MILE
Old Sacramento to Discovery Park

In order to get to the American River's Jedediah Smith Bicycle Trail from Old Sacramento, you'll be traveling for a mile on the **Sacramento River Bicycle Trail** located riverside of the railroad tracks by the Sacramento Discovery Museum. Take the time to read the interpretive signs describing the waterfront and the prison ship, the ***La Grange*** .

About 75 percent of all water flowing under the Golden Gate bridge first flows past Sacramento. Here is the river that carved the Golden Gate, nourished generations of native Americans, and carried many of the miners and settlers who built the foundations of the Sacramento you see today.

Up the trail is the I Street bridge, the fifth structure to span the Sacramento River at this location. Built in 1911, this double-decker bridge is California's heaviest movable bridge and is one of the country's busiest freight railroad links. It's always an event when the bridge opens to allow a big barge or boat to pass.

As you move upriver, cottonwood, alder and, valley oak trees provide shade and respite from city streets.

SACRAMENTO HISTORY AND SCIENCE ARCHIVE

Sacramento in 1857. Old American River channel and bridge.

You are near the site of the **old American River channel**. Here in the early 1850s, a ferry plied the mouth of the American River. In 1868, the old river mouth was filled in and the present channel dredged a half mile north of here.

About a quarter-mile up the trail, note the foundations on the river side of the path. The Sacramento waterfront was once lined with warehouses. Jibboom Street, parallel to the trail, was lined with bars and brothels during the Gold Rush period. Its name came from the "jibs and booms" of the sailing vessels docked along the river.

Up the way is the old **PG&E powerhouse**. The building, currently owned by the city of Sacramento, will be renovated into an enlarged home for the Discovery Museum Science and Space Center, now on Auburn Blvd.

A plaque at the trail's end commemorates Captain Tiscornia. The land his family gave to the city in his memory is a crucial link between the Sacramento and American River Parkways, and Two Rivers trail on the south side of the American River.

Next is the **Jibboom Street Bridge**. Reassembled here in 1929, this concrete and iron bridge once allowed cars to shuttle between Oakland and Alameda. Cut into pieces and carried by barge to Sacramento, the bridge was originally built as a swing-span bridge to allow river traffic up the American River. It served commuters until 1968 when the new I-5 bridge took over the job. A long trestle across Bannon Slough once connected the bridge to the Garden Highway.

From the bridge, watch the blue-green American River join with the silt-laden, brownish Sacramento River. Beginning on Mt. Shasta, the Sacramento River winds through large agricultural areas, draining much of the northern part of the state. The three forks of the American River cut through deep rocky canyons from the Sierra crest to the east and join at the valley's edge upriver from Folsom Dam. Leaving its small accumulation of silt behind the dam, the river then spills down to the Sacramento. Before hydraulic gold mining was outlawed in 1884, mining debris and silt washed out of the hills forming an almost impassable barrier at this junction.

The Lower American River is a designated "Recreational River" under the California Wild and Scenic Rivers Act (1972) and the National Wild and Scenic Rivers Act (1980). These distinctions give extra protection to the river's outstanding values. The trail provides access to Two Rivers Trail in Tiscornia Park on the south side of the American before it crosses the Jibboom Street Bridge to the American River Parkway and the Jedediah Smith Bicycle Trail.

NISENAN—NATIVE CALIFORNIANS

Valley Nisenan, southern members of the larger Maidu Indian tribe, lived along the American River, which they called *Kum Sayo*, "Roundhouse River," until about 1890. They were expert hunters, gatherers and fishermen, known for their effective fishing nets and the beauty of their feather cloaks and woven baskets. The bounty of the area and their resourcefulness is reflected by the absence of a starvation theme in their ancient stories.

Nisenan elder.

At the center of the Nisenan diet was the acorn (*ooti*), supplemented by seeds, roots, berries, fruit, worms, insects, meat from small mammals, deer, elk, antelope, shellfish and fish. Salmon were often speared or caught in a small weir in the river and dried for winter use. To collect food, they sometimes used small boats made by lashing together tules or by hollowing out logs. Cooking was usually done by dropping hot stones into stews or porridges held in tightly woven baskets of willow, redbud, sedge roots and ferns.

From late fall to early spring Nisenan gathered together in their villages. As the Earth awoke in spring, many villagers would migrate to the foothills to search for food and to trade with other tribes. In this way, Nisenan lived for thousands of years before settlers appeared. One of the first of these newcomers was Jedediah Smith, who reported the area's fortune in furs to the Hudson's Bay Company. The company sent out trappers who unintentionally brought diseases against which the natives had little immunity. Approximately 75% of the Nisenan population were killed by an 1833 malaria epidemic. By the time John Augustus Sutter arrived to build his fort in 1839, Nisenan could no longer guard their land.

About three hundred Nisenan worked for Sutter harvesting wheat. They lived in a small settlement on what is now the Southern Pacific Railroad yard. Others retreated farther into the foothills toward Coloma, site of the gold discovery. The invading miners killed many natives and decimated the game, grasslands, and forests Nisenan depended on for sustenance. For the first time in history, the remaining Nisenan were faced with starvation.

Today an active group of Nisenan survivors is dedicated to keeping the old culture alive. Replicas of elements of a Nisenan village and books about Nisenan culture are available at the Effie Yeaw Nature Center in Ancil Hoffman Park, Carmichael. For more information visit the State Indian Museum next to Sutter's Fort at 27th and K Streets.

RANDY SMITH

Willow and tule hut at the Effie Yeaw Nature Center.

"CAPTAIN" JOHN AUGUSTUS SUTTER

John Sutter is one of history's most intriguing characters. In 1834, he fled Switzerland, leaving behind his family to face his creditors. He embarked on a five-year, 20,000 mile quest that took him halfway around the world. By July of 1839, the persuasive and charming Sutter, a self-proclaimed captain in the Swiss infantry, was armed with cannons, ten Hawaiians "given" to him by King Kamehameha, and permission to establish a Mexican land grant. He soon departed Yerba Buena (San Francisco) with two small schooners and an additional crew of mercenaries.

SACRAMENTO HISTORY AND SCIENCE ARCHIVES

John Augustus Sutter

After restlessly probing uncharted rivers in the heart of the wilderness and narrowly avoiding a mutiny, they sailed up the American River as far as the summer's low water allowed. This spot, three miles from the confluence of the American and Sacramento Rivers, would be his "New Helvetia" (New Switzerland).

The choice turned out to be highly advantageous. For eons, periodic floods had dropped their loads of silt, creating fertile plains for farming. The American River would provide access to the timber and minerals of the foothills and waterpower for saw and grist mills. The Sacramento River would provide an easy route to distribute his products and obtain supplies.

Despite debt and a drought which hindered his wheat crops, as "don" of the Sacramento Valley, Sutter was quick to offer provisions and employment to new arrivals who could help settle the territory. Within ten years, Sutter and his small colony had begun many of the major endeavors for which California became known–wheat, cattle, fisheries, vineyards, tanning and lumber.

The life they carved out for themselves changed radically in 1848 when one of Sutter's employees, James Marshall, found a gold nugget at Sutter's sawmill in Coloma. One of the largest voluntary migrations in human history began, causing the downfall of Sutter's empire. The genial, expansive, but unscrupulous, young Sutter had been transformed by relative prosperity and respect into a fairly honest and complacent man—and it proved his undoing. New Helvetia went from a sleepy outpost to a bustling, chaotic community. Within months, his lands were overrun, cattle were killed, and wheat was trampled or stolen.

Sutter spent the rest of his life in a struggle with declining fortune, relative obscurity, and fruitless claims for government compensation. He died in 1880 and was buried near his final home in Lititz, Pennsylvania. The Sacramento we know today is built from his lost empire.

Sutter's Fort was in ruins by the late 1800s but still drew visitors such as these picnicking Victorian ladies. Today a rebuilt Sutter's Fort remains a popular destination.

History of the American River Parkway

In 1837, the Mexican Governor of California, Juan Bautista Alvarado, named the American River *El Río de los Americanos* because of the foreign trappers of "revolutionary" proclivities who tramped along its shores. Today, the American River Parkway is a model for urban river development in the United States, with an estimated five million visits each year. Among the recreational opportunities the Parkway provides are fishing, boating, rafting, picnicking, sunbathing, swimming, birdwatching, and, of course, biking and hiking.

Parkway and Trail Development

1915 The American River Parkway concept was first visualized by John Nolen.

1930s and 1940s Frederick Law Olmsted, master landscape architect, suggested a Parkway system for the American River.

1950 The City Council acquired eighty-two acres of land bordering Paradise Beach, one mile down river from H Street Bridge. Seventy–five acres of this land were donated by landowners John Sandburg and Louis Carlson.

1955 Completion of Folsom Dam meant floods no longer threatened riverfront land, and developers eyed the prime real estate.

1960 William Pond, the Sacramento County Park Department's first director, helped create a master plan that included the twenty-three miles of the American River Parkway from Discovery Park to Nimbus Dam. (The remaining nine miles of the Parkway from Nimbus Dam to Beals Point are under State jurisdiction). Bicycling enthusist Thomas MacBride (later a State Assemblyman and judge) furthered the idea of a bicycle trail through the Parkway.

1961 Despite the master plan, the County Planning Commission approved a subdivision within 125 feet of the river. The Save the American River Association (SARA) was formed and raised funds through programs such as "Elbow Room" in which squares of land were "sold" to the public but held by the county.

1960s and 1970s Specially reduced land prices, passage of county and state bonds, grants, and philanthropic donations allowed more private lands to be bought by the county. Bicycle trail miles grew. By 1967, land donations or easements from the Corey, Urrutia, and Johnson/Slobe families, allowed the Jedediah Smith Memorial Bicycle Trail to expand to six miles between Discovery Park and Cal Expo. Upriver, key parcels were sold or donated by the Teichert and Natomas companies and the family of Charles Goethe.

1980 The county bought the forty-two–acre parcel downstream from Arden Bar, allowing the two separate portions of the emerging bike trail to be linked at the Jedediah Smith/Harold Richey Memorial Trail Bridge.

1985 The current American River Parkway and almost thirty-two miles of bicycle trail were completed with the addition of the State–owned section from Nimbus Dam to Beals Point at Folsom Lake.

The Harold Richey Memorial Trail Bridge crosses the river between William B. Pond and River Bend Parks

REFERENCES

American River Natural History Association, *A History of the Lower American River, Prehistory to Parkway*, Peter J. Hayes, ed., 2005

American River Natural History Association, *The Outdoor World of the Sacramento Region*, Jo Smith and Peter J. Hayes, eds., 2004

Bakker, Elna, *An Island Called California*, University of California Press, Berkeley, California, 1972.

Barrows, Wray, *A History of Folsom*, The Folsom Historical Society, Folsom, California, 1994.

Burrill, Richard, *River of Sorrows*, Naturegraphs Publishers, Inc., Happy Camp, California, 1988.

Clarke, Charlotte Bringle, *Edible and Useful Plants of California*, University of California Press, Berkeley, California, 1977.

Dillon, Richard, *Fools Gold: A Biography of John Sutter*, Coward–McCann, New York, 1967.

Garvey, Stan, *King and Queen of the River.* River Heritage Press, Menlo Park, California, 1995.

Holden, William M., *Sacramento*, Two Rivers Publishing Co., Fair Oaks, California, 1988.

Kennedy, Des, *Nature's Outcasts-A New Look at Living Things We Love to Hate*, Story Communications, Inc., Pownal, Vermont, 1993.

Levy, Jo Ann, *They Saw the Elephant: Women in the California Gold Rush*, University of Oklahoma Press, Norman, Oklahoma, 1992.

Margolin, Malcolm, *The Way We Lived*, Heyday Books, Berkeley, California, 1981.

Mc Gowen, Joseph A., *History of the Sacramento Valley,* 2 Vols. Lewis Historical Publishing Co., New York and West Palm Beach, 1961.

Muir, John, *The Mountains of California,* (Originally published in Scribner's Monthly, February, 1878.)

Orr, Elizabeth L. and William N., *Rivers of the West, A Guide to the Geology and History,* Eagle Web Press, Eugene, Oregon, 1985.

Parsons, Mary Elizabeth, *The Wild Flowers of California –Their Names, Haunts and Habits,* California Academy of Sciences, San Francisco, California, 1960.

Pavlik, Bruce, Pamela Muick, Sharon Johnson and Marjorie Popper, *Oaks of California,* Cachuma Press and California Oak Foundation, Los Olivos, California, 1991.

Severson, Thor, *Sacramento–An Illustrated History:1839–1874.* California Historical Society, San Francisco, California, 1973.

Silver, Sue, *Folsom Fables: Pieces of the Past,* Victorian Secrets, Folsom, California, 1995.

Simpson, Richard, *OOTI–A Maidu Legacy*, Celestial Arts, Milbrae, California, 1977

Smith, Jedediah, *The Southwest Expedition of Jedediah S. Smith,* George R. Brooks, ed., University of Nebraska Press, Lincoln, Nebraska, 1977.

Sweet, Muriel, *Common Edible and Useful Plants of the West,* Naturegraph Publishers, Inc., Happy Camp, California, revised 1992.

Thompson, T., and Albert West, *Illustrated History of Sacramento County.* Oakland, California, 1880

Wilson, Norman L. and Arlene H. Towne, "Nisenan," *Handbook of North American Indians, Volume 8,* Robert Heizer, Ed. Smithsonian Institute, Washington D.C., 1978.

Winterstein, Herb, *Tales from Old Folsom,* Folsom Historical Society, Folsom, California 1981.

Overview Map of Current and Proposed Sacramento Area Bicycle Trails

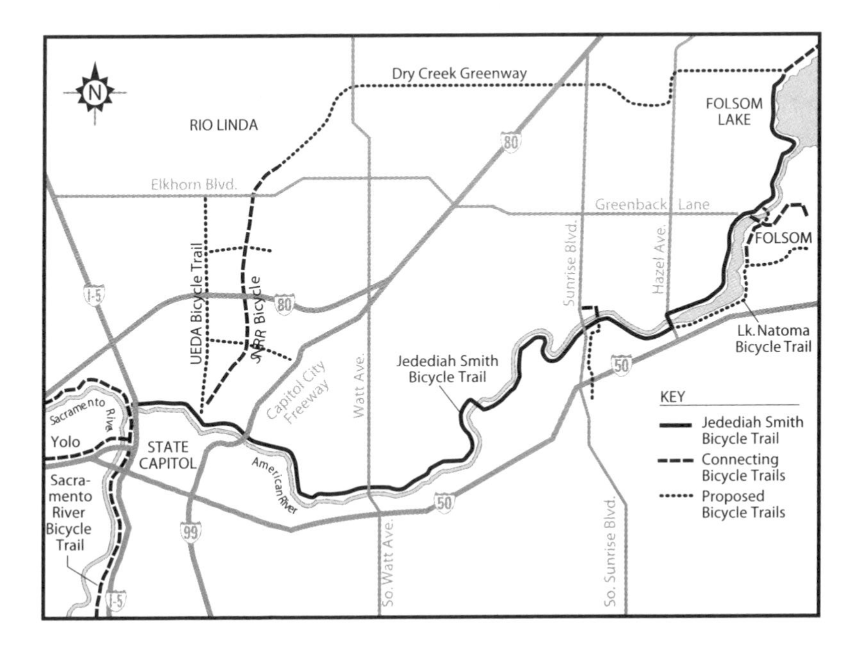

The Sacramento Northern and Ueda Bicycle Trails may join with a proposed Dry Creek Greenway Bicycle Trail which will connect with the Jedediah Smith Bicycle Trail–making a more than 60-mile loop. Trails south of Lake Natoma link with the Jedediah Smith Trail.

Animal Tracks and Nature Notes

INDEX

NOTE: Italicized page numbers beginning with "*I*" indicate photographs in the color photo insert section.